Daniel Hernández Osorio

WHEN IT´S TOO LATE TO LOVE

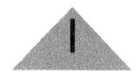

D'har Services
P.O. Box 290
Yelm, Wa 98597
info@dharservices.com
www.dharservices.com

Cover design: Xiomara Garcia
Cover image: Edilma Angel
Text design and layout: Nara

Original Title «Spanish»: Cuando para Amar es tarde

ISBN 13: 978-1-939948-26-7

Copyright © 2003, 2014 Daniel Hernández

Translated by : Sanako I. Hurtado

Second Edition 2104 «Improved»
First edition have sold over 10,000 copies

All rights reserved. No part of this publication may be reproduced in any form or by any means, electronic or mechanical, including photocopying, recording, or by any storage and retrieval system, without express permission in writing from the authors.

Printed in The United States

DEDICATION

To:

Angelica, my journey companion.

My sons, five gifts that I have received from heaven, and to whom I deeply thank for their existence.

Julio Daniel, who has taught me to be a wise dreamer.

Andrea Carolina, whose intelligence and sense of justice go beyond all expectations.

Juldy Roxana, a sweet and beautiful expression of God.

Maria Fernanda, whose character fills my heart with longing.

Arturo Hernandez, a light being filled with art and inspiration.

ACKNOWLEDGEMENTS

In the first place, I would like to mention my parents, Julio Daniel and Marina, my wife, my children and my siblings.

To all the people that contributed, directly or indirectly, to the publishing of this book.

To Richard Deeb, Flory Lobrinsky, Enrique Leal, Alex Padilla, John Roger, Waldo Alborta, Alan Frenk Lamm, Sigrid Effing, Rondal Fuchs, among others who, through their writings, seminars and conferences, have facilitated my immersion in this prodigious knowledge.

The possibility to investigate, comprehend, question, modify and appreciate the wonder of getting to live what one wants to live, I mostly owe it to the influence exercised upon me by all of those who decided to be my associates, clients and students. Especially to those who, while being in jail, were willing to listen, learn, experiment and better themselves. To witness their personal transformations has allowed me to cement the sense of my teachings.

Susana Nivia Gil, for her invaluable support in the process of editorial preparation.

Ana María Lozano, for compiling much of this information.

Luis Fánor Martinez, for his comments.

I thank you all for your support and giving of yourself in order to see this book materialized.

TABLE OF CONTENTS

Biography	XI
Prologue	XIII
Introduction	XV
PART I – Introspection	19
PART II – Confusion	25
PART III – Dialogues	35
PART IV – Knowledge	44
Rune 1 – God	45
Rune 2 – Purposes and dreams	50
Rune 3 – The law of Rang: Everything is possible	58
Rune 4 – The power of thought	62
Rune 5 – The power of the word	66
Rune 6 – The power of action	71
Rune 7 – Feelings and emotions	73
Rune 8 – The nourishment	76
Rune 9 – The breath	79
Rune 10 – Silence	81
Rune 11 – The sexual energy	83
Rune 12 – The flow of energy	86
Rune 13 – Forgiveness	90
Rune 14 – Creativity	93
Rune 15 – Attitude	95
Rune 16 – Leadership	98
Rune 17 – Communication	101
Rune 18 – Discipline	104
Rune 19 – Honesty	108
Rune 20 – Time	111
Rune 21 – Excellency	114
Rune 22 – I win, you win	116
Rune 23 – The power of association	118
Rune 24 – The power of goals	121
Rune 25 – Prosperity	124

Rune 26 – The law of acceptance	129
Rune 27 – The law of vibration	132
Rune 28 – The law of cycles	135
Rune 29 – The law of focus	139
Rune 30 – The law of polarity	142
Rune 31 – The law of Karma and Dharma or Cause and effect	145
Rune 32 – The law of reversibility	151
Rune 33 – The law of synchronicity	155
Rune 34 – Light and shadow	159
Rune 35 – First day	165
Rune 36 – Second day	168
Rune 37 – Third day	170
Rune 38 – Fourth day	172
Rune 39 – Fifth day	174
Rune 40 – Sixth day	176
Rune 41 – Seventh day	178
Rune 42 – To work in the light	181
Rune 43 – The new age	187
Rune 44 – Death	194
Rune 45 – Twin souls	198
Rune 46 – Physical immortality	201
Rune 47 – The power of love	205
Rune 48 – The supreme blessing	209
Part V – Enlightenment	213
End of the dialogues	214
Rebirth	220
Waking up	221
A note from the author	224

DANIEL HERNANDEZ OSORIO

Considered one of the most renowned Latin American speakers in the area of self-improvement, Daniel Hernandez Osorio is a public accountant graduated from the *Pontificia Universidad Javeriana of Bogotá*, Colombia, where he has been teaching Excellence Models. Schooled in Santiago de Chile as master and trainer in Neuro-linguistic Programming. He took the series of seminars "Insight" levels I – IV recognized by the *University of Santa Monica* in California, USA.

A professional in Rebirthing, Creative Thought and Cellular Programming from the *Rebirthing Association of Spain*. He took courses in PhotoReading, Activating your Success, and Mind Mapping from the *Colegio de Investigación y Desarrollo Empresarial* in Mexico.

Mr. Hernandez Osorio has received training in several self-knowledge techniques: Psychodrama, Enneagram, Gestalt, Music Therapy, Hypnosis, Reiki, Mental Power, Macrobiotics, Catharsis, Transcendental Meditation, and Action and Project Management.

He was a radio host and T.V. and radio producer.

Teaches leadership, creativity and communication with emphasis on personal responsibility at several Colombian prisons, as part of his social labor.

Worked in the rehabilitation of combat wounded military personal for the health battalion in Bogotá, Colombia.

Mr. Hernandez Osorio is a successful businessperson in the building of consumer communities or networking. His ample knowledge in the subject has allowed him to train many business employees in several countries around the world. He is the President of the Colombian branch of a distinguished company in the world of Interactive Commerce training.

Noted business consultant for various Latin American companies, he trains professionals in all areas in the principles of success, whom are able to verify the efficacy of what they learn through the undeniable improvement in the quality of their lives, as well as their businesses.

Daniel Hernandez is the creator of three powerful series of seminars in the area of personal development. These are:

1. Self-Knowledge

2. To be born to Love

3. Excellence Models

The seminars are aimed at providing individuals with the tools to better know themselves, to recognize and transform their personal limitations; to learn and to apply principles of success in their lives.

The author invites you to immerse yourself in the book, *When it's too late for love*, a compilation of principles of success that, not only will it captivate you, but will inspire you to persevere and do whatever it takes in order for you to conquer your dreams, with clarity on your objectives and inner strength.

PROLOGUE

I felt honored when my father asked me to write the prologue to his first book, for this is a manual in human excellence.

The person who writes the prologue of a book is usually some kind of master of its content; sort of an expert in the subject or genre. However, I only learned from it and this may be your case as well. It is only after I say this that I actually feel comfortable to share with you this feeling in the presence of the dilemma of having to write this prologue.

Thanks to my mother I received a Christian education, and with time I have devised my own system to evaluate the information that I receive, as well as my beliefs.

I grew up in America, a society of very different cultures, races and values, and along with my mother's teachings, I have learned to elevate myself and derive information beyond any judgment.

In my opinion, if what you think and practice on a day-to-day basis affects your life in a positive way, then please go on with it. Because of this, I suggest that you extract and adapt the information contained in this book which you consider will have a positive impact in the construction of your life.

With this book, my father – who is well versed in many lines of thought – transmits to the reader a share of the knowledge he has acquired and applied throughout his own journey. "When it's too late to Love," is a journey filled with experiences and lessons that will serve as a guide towards the understanding of love and the reunification with the divine within you. It also contains an excellent vision on the importance of being in communion with our essence.

So when I thought about what to write, I realized the explanation my father gave me about the meaning of the title of the book is well reflected in the experience I was having right at that moment in my life. Like many others, I also heard - several times - that "it is never too late for love." But right at that moment I was living what previous experience had revealed to my father: that the moment to love is the present, and turning back time and acting at the right moment – whether it is to write a prologue or to do something else we left for later – is not possible. The logical outcome is the realization that you did not love in the moment, and you will never be able to love in that moment because that moment is gone.

It is important to understand this, not to become depressed about a past I believe should stay where it belongs, but rather in order to comprehend how significant it is the fact we have the option to love now, to live with love and to put love in everything we do.

When you finish reading this book, you will know many of the complex and not-so-complex traps that human beings set up for themselves, such as: unawareness of their full potential, procrastinating, ignorance of natural laws, conformity, etc.

In the end, I chose to make mine - and I invite you to make yours – the many lessons contained in this book, and continually work to become a better being. Please be clear that none of the many written theories and philosophies can do anything for you unless you decide to put them into practice.

In that sense, this book provides us with the tools which allow us to love everything and everyone from this moment on...before it is too late to do it.

God blesses you,

Julio Daniel Hernández T. III

INTRODUCTION

The shortest, yet the longest road to walk is the one that leads us from our heads and into our hearts; forty centimeters of distance and entire lives to tread it.

To learn to go beyond our skin in order to find the very essence of things, a sacred space without judgments or maps, a place where the being is filled, omnipotent, omnisapient and omnipresent, without any limits, except the self-imposed ones. That is the journey that this book invites you to live.

However, just as the master only appears when the student is ready, and there is a myriad of events that happen to him before and after the master's appearance in order to test whether he deserves the encounter, or maybe the student is tested in the end in order to verify that he has learned his lessons, so this book endeavors to face you with two of the most important and magical moments in your life.

The first one is a filter so that only the one that is ready will be able to nurture himself with the elixir of wisdom; the second one is a confirmation that you are ready to give a step toward your excellence.

The title of the book will be the first filter, and you are mistaken if you believe that you are holding in your hands a sentimental love story, this will be your first test to confirm whether you are ready to travel from your head and into your heart. The second magical moment will be an awakening that will lead you to the conquest of your own self and your dreams.

In June of 2001, during a trip to the United States of America with the occasion of my daughter Andrea's graduation, I took the opportunity to work more intensely on this book. Once back in Colombia, a computer virus erased all of my documents and I found myself, again, with a dream within my hands and the whole road ahead of me, because writing is such a task that in many cases prevents you from moving ahead with any other areas of your life.

I reflected upon it. I made up many excuses. I thought I would not have the availability of time in order to do it, and as such, it would be very difficult to start all over again. Hence, I desired to write a book about the significance of giving ourselves the time do the things in life that we considered to be important, about the commitment to our dreams, about having perseverance and constancy in the pursuit of our goals and about living life with courage, faith, enthusiasm and love. However, despite having so many wishes, I always came up with a good excuse in order to give up and not persevere.

Many transformative ideas end up being forgotten out of our custom to give up in the face of obstacles, and because we forget that, we came here to become a better person, to learn the lessons as a result of overcoming such obstacles.

How many may have dreamed of going to the moon before a few decided to give it a try and make that dream possible? How many would have tried to fly before the Wright brothers? How many may have thought about the roundness of the Earth before Christopher Columbus discoveries? How many people, before the time of Christ, knew that everything could be achieved with love?

It is common to come across people bestowed with many gifts, aptitudes and qualities, yet their lives are a failure because they have the bad habit of not acting and lack perseverance in the search for what they wish. I was faced with the same dilemma that millions of people face at every moment of their existence: To persist or to give up. And before I was even conscious of the decision I made, I found myself sitting in front of the computer writing once more "When is too late for love," right after having a dream that would forever change my life.

You will find wisdom in the peace of your soul, and the transformation of a day in the dawn of the aurora; days of love and light, days of darkness and hopelessness, and the best is... You get to choose!

In the days when the forgotten was still remembered, and the day and night made no difference, there lived a man used to delay things and incapable of completing his dreams. He lived his life in the incoherence between what he knew he was capable to achieve, and the results he obtained from applying the wrong principles and strategies of life.

The main character of this story lives the daily dilemma most of us live; hence, this is my story and your story as well, though neither one of us lived it.

PART I

INTROSPECTION

What would happen if you knew, with all certainty, that the book of life is already written and today is your last day on the planet? What would you do? ... Please, whatever that is, do it now. In the words of Ernest Hemingway, "don't ask for whom the bell tolls," better, be diligent! For the next ones may toll for you.

* * *

I was really exhausted; too many thoughts going through my mind. The incomplete part of my days, all the broken promises, abandoned goals and issues I had just started, they all made me feel excessively tired. I once heard that when we do not close a cycle or leave something incomplete, that it creates a waste of energy which makes one feel really tired even if one is not doing anything. Meaning, it is not about doing something that makes you feel tired, but it is about having unfinished business; even more, it has been proven that to engage in a lot of activities prepares us for more activities, and it allows us to tap into a wonderful source of inner energy we cannot even fathom.

In the pale green wall opposite to the living room, the old wooden clock marked 1:15 in the afternoon. After lunch, I made myself ready to take a nap in the couch, which now looked more comfortable than ever. I fell asleep like a baby in a cradle, in that ritual of pleasure which had become a routine since quite a long time, maybe since I stopped working for others, a moment I still recall.

It was not I who decided to leave. On the contrary, on the day I was laid, off all of my fears came to the surface and I felt the world crumble. Today, I cannot thank the heavens enough for such an event; it was a decision that, even though I could not make on my own at the time, my heart wished for it. I wanted to quit my job for quite a while; the apprehensions, the fear to be free and the responsibility that comes with it, it all gave me the perfect excuse to justify the reason I kept delaying making the decision on my own. Like Shakespeare said: "There is a divinity that shapes our ends, rough–hew them how we will." The universe made the decision for me, it put me out on the road and I ventured to write my own story. Life took charge – like it always does – and it made my authentic, inner heart desires come true.

I endeavored to enjoy my fifteen minutes of rest; I will have so much to do that the best thing I could do was to recover my energies. Many times, as I rested, I thought I had solved some of the many unfinished issues. It is contradicting, wanting to sleep for a while in order to recover, to forget about our reality for a moment, and then later realize that our dream has turned into a nightmare which expresses our inability to finish our pending business. On some occasions, I even woke up trembling and sweating, though it usually happened when I was sleeping at night, but rarely during naps.

This time everything was different. All of a sudden, I was invaded by a profound sense of peace and a feeling of love I had never experienced before, a joy and desire to live; above all, an imperative need to complete the so many unresolved issues in my life. I promised myself I would go back to each one of them and finish them one by one. I was filled with power, strength and determination. I reviewed all of my life, and I was able to see clear images of every transcendental moment; for example, the day I promised to write a book. But I also witnessed myself coming up with truck loads of apologies in order to justify why I was delaying it: "Today I am not inspired, the muses are not speaking to me," "I am too busy," "tomorrow will be a better day," and it continued this way day after day, until the moment came when the illusion of it just died and I heard myself saying I just did not have the vocation to write.

Human beings can come up with infinite ways to undermine their own power, which I understand today to be unlimited. Maybe we cannot realize that those white lies and the liberties we take actually make us weak, betray our dreams and leave us without hope. Many times, I told my college students that behind every excuse therein lies a mediocre person «someone who half–believes»; behind a small excuse, a small mediocre; behind a big excuse, a bigger mediocre.

It could have been very different if I had just engaged in the necessary actions. Yes, the action.

In the action lies the secret, the magic word that makes possible the impossible, the abracadabra of our realizations. Why should we ignore that it is *action* what turns us into masters, that it set us apart from the valley of illusion and fantasy and brings us to the valley of hope and fullness? In the performance of any art, it is well known that it is repetition what builds a reputation, and such repetition is produced by action. To be clear about what one wants, the successful outcome of our endeavor, and to perform the actions that will lead us to the result – coupled with a constant adjustment of the direction – is one of the easiest ways to achieve success in any project one undertakes.

It would be ideal if in the face of every dream, every project or idea, we would have the determination to act on it. I do not remember very well, but somewhere I read that it is not that inspiration strikes and then the painter picks up his brush and begins the construction of his art; on the contrary, when the painter holds the brush and begins to paint his work of art, that is when inspirations comes. Now I clearly understand it. Action, action, action, and then inspiration will follow us in everything we endeavor to do; because muses are way too busy in order to lose their time with those who lack certainty within their hearts. The purpose of all knowledge is to inspire us into action.

During my after–nap reflections, some other clear memories rushed back to my mind, and with each one of them I found myself feeling the deep need to act on it. I realized there is no point in delaying things, and I promised myself to systematically go back to every single thing and finish it. I had never felt something so clearly; it was all decided; from this day on, I would be a new man and I knew this would be a great source of empowerment. The feeling grew stronger by just planning how to close each cycle, and a great source of energy began to flow from within me.

When I got out of the couch after the nap, the day light seem brighter. I had a greater sense of the present moment, and like never before, I felt a tremendous desire to live and act. The rays of sun fell dimly through the window and my body temperature was warmer than usual. In front of me, a painting of the Last Supper hanging on the wall reminded me of my childhood; something allowed me see the atmosphere clearer and brighter. I wanted to leave behind all my comforts and throw myself into action. In such a short amount of time for pondering and resting, it was very clear to me that the key to life lies in immediate action and fulfilling the commitments made to ourselves and to others. Getting up from the couch I noticed I felt lighter than usual. In my internal dialogue, I was telling myself such was the magical feeling which came as a result of making a decision.

In summary, I was more happy and aware. All of a sudden, in the midst of that strange yet pleasant sensation, I felt the urgent need to look back, toward the couch, and when I did I felt a surge of intense cold air running through my body: I saw myself...yes, there I was, laying in the couch, uncomfortable, pale and rigid. I was so surprised that I yelled at the top of my lungs in utter confusion; it was such a loud yell that it inundated the living room and threatened with shattering the window glass, but nobody could hear me. I knew I was dead, but I did not want to admit it. Once again, it was too late for love, this time to love life.

"Life, like Earth, is round; you walk so much that in the end you arrive at the same place."
Daniel Hernández.

"When Pedro left that morning, he did not know. Oh, beloved soul! That the light of that morning was the light of his last day."
Silvio Rodríguez.

PART II

CONFUSION

I felt confusion, rejection and I wished for this experience to be nothing more than a nightmare, nothing real. I wanted to wake up in tranquility, as if I had just had a dream. However, this was not the case; I had stayed in the land of dreams, and as I looked at my motionless body I felt the desire to never return to it. Nevertheless, I did want to go back to the experience of being alive, to what I thought being alive meant. Never before had I been so consciously aware, nor had I lived in the present with such sense of fullness and energy. My body, not the one laying in the couch, but the one through which I now lived and felt – and which I surely used every night while asleep – that body was more youthful and filled with vitality than ever before.

Someone entered the living room, saw me lying on the couch and asked me to wake up because it was beginning to get late. "Late for what?" I wondered. The person reproached me that I was not making the best of my day, and this was not the time of the day to be sleeping – as he shook my shoulders – and with an even louder voice he yelled at me. The person was beginning to panic. Until finally he yelled, "He is dead!" When the person turned, I realized it was my wife. Ultimately, our relationship was not going well; for some time already, she had stopped believing in me. She witnessed me starting many projects but never finishing any of them, yet she still loved and accepted me. Thanks to her love and acceptance she had the expectation that, somehow, one day I would transform into the person I promised to be every morning.

Everything was chaos: the phone was ringing; she was making phone calls, people arriving at my house – how ironic to say my house, when now I could not even touch it! –. I watched the sadness in the faces of the family members who were arriving, and I wanted to shout and tell them I was more alive than ever. I tried to touch them but they could not feel me. Some men came rushing in with a gurney, and as they passed in front of me, I could not feel them; it seemed as if they had gone through me. I realized I could perfectly hear what people were saying, but I could not touch anything. I was only able to connect with that body via sight and hearing. Not with the eyes and ears of the other body which I rejected ever more, but with my body that was equal to that, but, was not that one. It was like a duplicate of it, yet better, enhanced, lighter and more subtle. Everything was happening really fast, and I had the same sensation I experienced when I went to the movie theater; I used to feel like a lot of time had passed, like days or years, while my wrist watch indicated the movie had lasted only two hours.

Tears, desolation, a lot of confusion and rejection. That is all I could observe. They took that body which I insisted in denying was mine; they dressed it up, applied some make up and placed it in a coffin. What a scene!

Some time ago, during a self improvement workshop, an instructor said that at the time of death we would be able to hear everything happening around us, and this would be purgatory. Now I knew it was true. This sensation I was experiencing was a living purgatory! The instructor also said that the more we were willing to follow our own path, and not be attached to what we call life, that it would help to make the process less painful. His recommendations were:

we will see a light we should follow – according to him – and to act as if we were waking up from a dream; it would be ridiculous to continue dreaming the same, so it is best to be willing to live a new day in order to have a new dream.

Even though it all sounded very logic, now that I was in the midst of the situation, I did not want to wake up; a part of me could not accept it. The more I rejected the situation, the more suffering I felt inside my heart, and his words were beginning to come true; I would go through my own purgatory. I remembered the words of the instructor: "If you wish to stop suffering you must let go of the need to perpetuate the past, and surrender to the certainty that everything which will come next will be better than what you have lived so far." However, how could I give up the so many experiences I had lived?

Under the circumstances I decided to ponder, and remembered that many times during the course of my life I had already died in many situations, and that I created suffering every time I could not accept the fact my time to share with someone or live a certain experience was already finished; until I finally accepted it and recognized that no matter what, I could not stop time.

Yes, many times in my life I had already died. For example, when I wished to return to my home city after 20 years of absence, the house where we used to live no longer existed. I went to the house which belonged to a friend of mine, and through a window, a white hair lady told me he had gotten married and now lived in a far away city. I felt sad; his mother did not remember me and did not even open the door for me. On another occasion, I refused to accept the end of a relationship with the woman who was my girlfriend at the time; years later, I coincided with her at a shopping mall and I could not remember her name. She had also died inside of me. Even if I wanted to recover those moments, it was not possible. Perhaps we die in life at every moment!

A female poet friend of mine, Constanza de Samper, wrote once: "I live my life dying in moments, I die in life and in death I live, living is dying in thousands of ways and an awakening after thousands of deaths."

I took a deep breath; I closed my eyes and refused to continue to live this experience. I could recognize that embedded within this decision was my own farewell; a farewell to my own self from that dream, from that life, from that past, from everything. The decision was made, it was time to continue my journey and leave behind the entire story. All of a sudden, a light enveloped me; I could not feel anything and my heart was swelling with happiness. What a sensation! Never before was there so much love in my heart. It was like being face to face with someone greater than me, with the light, with God, with the very essence of things.

During the self–improvement workshop, we were warned that at the time of death we would come face to face with God, regardless of our beliefs. If someone believed in Buddha, he would find himself in front of Buddha; if he believed in Christ, he would find himself in front of Christ; if he believed in Muhammad, he would be in front of Muhammad; if he believed in the Virgin Mary, he would see her; if he believed in some saint, he would see such saint. Someone asked what would happen if someone did not believe in anyone, the instructor answered that the person would feel the presence of something superior, and he or she would see the light, because God who is everything can turn into the image that we had of Him in life as we searched for our own divinity.

Fullness and omnipresence enveloped me. I felt like crying, not of sadness, but this time out of happiness and love for what was pouring from me. I felt welcomed, loved and accepted. I could certainly recognize that I was with God, in God, and that maybe I had never been apart from Him. For an instant, I imagined I might be judged, evaluated or condemned; in reality what I felt was acceptance, and all the chains from my past were erased from my thoughts. I do not know how much time passed, it seemed like forever, and truthfully I did not want to leave this experience…and there again I was forgetting that attachment is a sure way to create suffering, and that to flow, to trust the change and expect the best at every new moment is the right way to have faith and believe in God. I repeated to myself several times that everything happens for my own good, that anything which persistently remains is that to which we resist, and pain is the price to pay for resisting life.

I began to understand change is inevitable, and I discovered I was surrounded by many friends who had passed before me; some of them appeared on previous dreams or, as it is usually called, in other lives. The expressions on their faces were of understanding, and their attitude was a welcoming one. I could not resist the urge to explode with laughter, for I felt filled, and the laughter came from deep within my soul. Immediately, I knew two things: one, that experiences in the land of the dead – which from now on I will call the fourth dimension – are so intense or superior to those of the land of the living – which from now on I will call the third dimension – that I believe this fourth dimensional world is where we go to when we fall asleep, maybe so we do not forget from where we came. And second, I learned that in the fourth dimension it is impossible to communicate through sounds or words – so far at least – for it is all about energy.

Every person radiated energy from their body, of different colors and intensity; I completely understood them, even though I did not know when I had learned the language. Immediately, I noticed every time my thoughts shifted they changed the color and intensity of my own energy. Something told me we communicate in the same way in the third dimension, yet the majority of us loses the capacity to see and interpret those energies mainly because our hearts are not pure enough to connect with such knowledge; this prevents us from communicating with fairies or angels, and awaken ourselves to the deeper knowledge, the one which is only told to us through children stories. For men, it would be worthless to posses all of that knowledge because he would not understand it, and if he did, he would surely use it in order to manipulate others.

I do not know how much time passed while I lived this experience, but what I did notice was that my perception of time was changing; now it appeared to be slower, or maybe I perceived it in this way because I was more conscious of the details. I continued to see that my body, just as the one I had in the third dimension, looked better and younger.

All of a sudden, in less than a heartbeat, I found myself in a parallel world whose reality mimicked the third dimension to the 'T'. Again, it was an enhanced version of the Earth. There were great cities with better technology; many people walking and crossing the streets and avenues, going to houses and buildings of diverse architecture. Everyone knew where they were going. I observed many beings who – just as me – had just arrived to this parallel world, to this place where many people seem to come and go to on a constant basis; it all seemed curious to me, and I remembered that it is the same in the third dimension. The place was diverse and beautiful. To me, the atmosphere of peace and respect was a novelty; everybody was too busy completing something as to bother with interrupting or troubling someone else.

I arrived to a place I thought I had been to before. A part of me knew I had to go directly to this place, same as when you get back to the home from where you have been absent for a long time and you know exactly where everything is. I noticed the life styles were very different. However, nobody complained about their own; even I, a newcomer to this world, understood this lifestyle was the one I deserved and corresponded to my level of evolution or learning. I also understood the third dimension is a place that we go to in order to evolve. Yes, the differences in the fourth dimension were large, yet nobody envied anyone; the quality of life of any one person was respected and admired, and it was understood that the better it was, it was because the person had a greater level of evolution. Everybody had what he or she deserved for what they had done in life. Now I understood the teaching from the instructor: the experience is more complete, something never lived before; is being in front of God, and this happens consciously at the time of death.

I became conscious; I had moved to another place, a great city, a place which had been pre—established by me. I met with some friends, who had died before me, and we were able to communicate once again. They welcomed me, and their faces showed mercy toward my being, like when you receive someone who has just gone through a rough experience. They expressed their love and acceptance toward me; no body judged me; they simply watched me as if already knowing the best was yet to come; their eyes expressing a form of silent congratulation. Nonetheless, I felt incomplete, like something was missing and I wanted to know what it was; I had the feeling I was going to be evaluated, that the moment had arrived, to answer for what I had done in life. I felt scared, I wanted to escape.

I knew I had not accomplished every single thing I desired, and I had left many unfinished business; besides, I would have liked to be conscious of the fact that, what I called life is actually "not real," and avoid falling into the trap of that illusion. It was too late for regrets, tough. I understood this happens to every mortal, we all know we are going to die, but nobody accepts the fact that they could be the next one in line. When death strikes most of us are taken by surprise, rendering us unable to pack our bags or repair the damage we have inflicted upon others throughout our lives. It seems as if pretending to not know when our turn to die is, is part of the game called life. The wisest ones prepare themselves to die every day, and at the same time, to live.

During the course of this reflection, the light came upon me once more; it felt pretty impressive to be alone there, in the midst of everything, and even more, to be all. Again, I felt that full, inexpressible feeling. I saw myself there, in front of Him, with the image I used to hold of what God looked like; a beautiful face which embodied everything, the purity, the wisdom and the love I never saw in any human face, but yet at the same time was my face. I could not understand why the face of God was my own face. It was like contemplating yourself as the reflection of a perfect being in a mirror, but with the same physical traits; that other me reflected complete love, light, purity, justice, honesty, wisdom, humility and many other sacred feelings. I looked at myself with so much tenderness and understanding that my throat was completely closed; I could not speak or make a sound. All I ever searched for in life was a way to be like that, the perfected version of us that we all carry within. Now I understood why the greatest answers to my worries always came from within me. This was the confirmation to one of my deepest beliefs: God and I are one, and the purpose of life is to uncover the unlimited being that we all carry within, or better, which we always are and from whom we are never apart.

This must be the reason humans have the need to set goals that go beyond their limits, allowing them to encounter, in the obstacles, opportunities to advance. People who do not seek to better themselves, who have no goals, challenges or dreams, begin to die; maybe the reason for living lies in recognizing that everything is possible. My theory was being proved, and in that moment in front of God I needed to calm down, because this time He would have to listen to me and answer some questions.

I asked myself if maybe this was just another illusion, if maybe I was just in front of another one of my own mental creations, and if what I saw was just what I wanted to see. Suddenly I heard a voice, sweeter than the most beautiful melody I had ever heard, and it said to me:

"Hello! I am your most beloved, your guardian angel, your higher self, your God, I am you and you are Me; we are one and the same, and I am in you and you are in Me; together, we are a particle of perfection that belongs to the great universal current, almighty and eternal. I am here to guide you."

PART III

DIALOGUES

He could read my thoughts. It seemed as if everything that I am, had accomplished or ruined, He already knew. I was completely naked and exposed, just as I was. However, He did not judge me, and his look – on the contrary – was one of compassion, acceptance and understanding. After much hesitation, and being ridden with fears and doubts, I decided to speak with God, because until then He had respected my need for silence.

So, I said: *"Hello! It is strange that I want to speak with you, for I feel I speak to myself or to a more perfected part of me. Truthfully, who are you?"*

"Let us say that, for the purpose of your current stage of existence, I am your most beloved. And I call myself this because that is what you have done for me, you have loved me well. I am the part of you that you have wished to be and which, as you are about to understand, you already were. You just needed to recognize it."

"Where have you been all of this time?" I asked

"In you, or better said, you are in me and I am in All."

"In me? In you? In All?" I asked

*"I am your observer, and as such, you are that which I observe. In essence, you and I are one. This is the time to become conscious of the lessons learned. In this encounter,

you will be able to realize how much you learned in the stage you have just finished. You will make sense of many of the experiences you had, and you will understand many things. For now, I just want you to rest, get ready to receive some lessons you had wanted to learn and evaluate how much you were able to accomplish."

I fell into a deep sleep and it was like being alive again. I was the observed and at the same time the observer. As soon as I thought of something, I was there; if I thought of someone, the person would appear in order to share that experience with me. I thought about my wife and I saw her, in two different planes. In one, she appeared to be mourning, somewhat pale and disillusioned; in the other one, a parallel world, it seemed as if as we talked; we had the power to communicate through dreams. The same thing happened with my children and some friends. I played with this ability for a while, until it became a routine and, as a result, I was not that entertained by it anymore. I already knew the living and the dead could share when they dreamed of each other at the same time, which gave me a great sense of happiness, even though I had only experienced it for a short period of time. I could tell them many things; be with them, share and re–conquer the past. Although time passed at a pace different from that of the third dimension, I am sure I enjoyed the experience for a long time.

I felt a breath of fresh air running through my body, a strange smell which I recognized as sacred; I opened my eyes, and once more, I was in front of God. This time I could see something more than just his presence, a level of vibration where life turns into a real paradise. I could see the landscape. In the backdrop, in the distance, there was a big rainbow and multicolored gardens filled with beautiful flowers. The temperature was nice and the sun illuminated everything with its perfect light. Oh! How nice! At least I knew this place was majestically kept so that, when we arrived, we would have a comfortable place to wake up to from such an unexpected change.

I noticed, although much later in time, how delighted I was by every experience in such a manner which surpassed the limits of time and space, connecting me with eternity.

I looked up and saw how God stared at me. He looked at me in a way that made me feel secure and at ease. Two unusual emotions, especially when you think about all the time you wasted in life and the imminent moment of accountability. He looked at me again, with a look of tenderness, compassion and mercy that confirmed I was indeed in the presence of a saint. Oh! How I wished for Him to speak! He rarely did; every uttered word held a precise meaning. I perfectly remember the only question he asked: "Are you ready?" I just nodded in agreement, but what I really wanted to say was: "Ready for what?"

I was taken – I do not know how – to a beautiful place inhabited by amazing light beings who played and joked about mortals. I recognized many spiritual leaders and founders of many religions. I felt the desire to protest against the clear disparity between the two worlds: the third dimension, where people look for God in many ways and that, in most cases, remain confused and defend their beliefs as if they were the only one, the true one. On the other hand, there was this world where I was, where everyone was united. I felt it was somewhat of a mockery of humanity: Catholics, Christians, Jehovah's witnesses, Muslims, Shiites, Buddhists, Jews and many other men and women that were grouped into multiple religions which, attached to their beliefs, go about life attempting to teach their truth as if it was the only road to salvation; in many cases making enemies and giving rise to wars, conflicts and murder. But right at this place, without any apparent kind of problem, they were all sharing, all the leaders, like long time friends who get together while their followers waste their lives trying to bring more sheep to their flocks and preaching all over the place. Like it always used to happen whenever I was in disagreement with something or someone, I felt my blood boiling with anger and my face showed obvious signs of nonconformity in the lights of what appeared to be a very hypocritical situation. One of these beings smiled, and with a loud voice said:

"Here is another one who blames us for the separation that has been caused by the religious fanatics of humanity. None of us created any religion." He said, as he looked straight at my eyes. He continued, *"They were all created by our followers, who forgetting the essence of our teachings fell pray to spiritual pride – maybe one of the greatest of sins – and decided to appoint themselves as the holders of the truth. We do not inspire religions, but people with pure and clean hearts to be the channels of light beyond the religion they profess. In fact, if you wish to, you will discover that our teachings have always been the same, but expressed in different manners and according to the particular historical context of the moment for that generation. Even though each one of us chose a different point in time, the message always was, and is, the same: God is love. To learn to love is to learn to manifest the glory of God. Anything contrary to love must be healed. The power is in you and you will be able to awaken it with love. Even further, change the name each religion assigns to God for the word 'Love,' and you will understand that in essence all religions are telling the same. 'Religion' comes from the Latin word religare, which means 'union,' and the only thing*

which unites the world is love; just the unruly ego from a few, combined with the thirst for power of others, are creating separation and confusion on Earth." He finished by saying:

"Blessed is he who is joined by means of love with their brothers and succeeds in overcoming the need to persuade or be convinced, because he will be elected as a light channel."

After that, everything was silent. I went into a deep reflection. I became conscious of the meaning of the lesson; I had received one of the most important teachings and revelations that I could think of.

I sat down in a comfortable chair. In front of me, the great premiere of the movie of my life was about to be projected onto a big screen, a presentation to which the very main character had showed up in order to analyze every single detail, not from his ego, but from his own light. I immersed myself in the movie, and witnessed everything starting from the first day of my life when my mother and father first conceived me; the fetal phase inside my mother's womb, my birth, my childhood, and even the last day when I went to take that nap at 1:15 in the afternoon. The sensation is indescribable; with a knot in my throat, overtaken by fear, sweaty and with butterflies in my stomach, yet at the same time, I also felt a surge – from somewhere deep within me – of understanding, comprehension and acceptance. I remember I began to see how the causes and effects of each of the circumstances in my life became more congruent, logic and symmetric; they were all perfect, and the 'why' and 'what for' of every experience and person that I knew, somehow fit wonderfully all together.

I realized that in some instances of my life I missed the opportunity to engage key and important people and experiences who held a great deal of lessons to learn, lessons that would have been very useful in order to endure future experiences. Because I limited my learning, I had to learn the hard way, sort of like taking part in a competition for which I had not been previously prepared. I recognized as well that every experience contained within itself a lesson or a teaching, and when we fail to learn a lesson, the experiences continue to repeat over and over; as a result, instead of learning what was available to me, I would fall into repeating what seemed to be my favorite line: "Why me, again, my God? And, why me?" I also believed it was all a form of punishment; but sitting there, in front of the screen, I could see that was not the case. Maybe the right question to ask would have been: "What do I need to learn from this experience?" Because once the lesson is learned, the experiences change.

I also became aware of the fact that the greatest part of my life was spent in repetitions, and I thought it was such a waste and lack of creativity. Now I understood the reason for the existence of so many preachers and fortune tellers. I could so easily predict my thoughts and reactions to the next experience that I felt sorry for myself. Therefore, with much more understanding and clarity, I observed the passing of my whole life, the promises I left undone and how they vanished, and the truck loads of excuses. I understood that at several points in my life I experienced a surge of some strange kind of force arising from somewhere deep within me, which bid me to do the right thing. However, even though my heart could clearly recognize such force, my decisions lacked the necessary strength to allow me to choose the change and pursuit what I really wanted.

It was sad to evoke that distant afternoon, when I lay down on the couch after lunch ready to enjoy the long–

cherished dream of the siesta, without having the slightest suspicion I would never get up from that couch in order to continue with my story.

I thought about how many people must have gone through the same thing that happened to me on that day, at the very same time, but in different places. I remember thinking how very few people really take the time to prepare for death, and many just go about life wasting their time and dying in life. I thought surely somewhere, at that very same moment, someone was running out of time and death was catching them by surprise, when they least expected or desired it. Then, I fell into a deep silence, but this time I was filled with sadness, melancholy and a longing for something from my past that I could not put my finger on.

I lost track of how much time had passed; again, I felt the presence of God showing me that I needed to go into some cloisters where I would be shown forty–eight runes. Each one of these runes would present a lesson that I should have learned in life. It was simple, what we would do: go into each one of the cloisters, read the runes or lessons, and then examine my past, that same one I had the opportunity to live in the third dimension and which I re–lived when I was seating, watching the projection of the movie of my own life. I knew at the end of each rune I would find a test that, if I had engaged it in the third dimension, it would have meant I had indeed learned that particular lesson. This would allow me to know how many lessons I had actually learned throughout my life, which was reflected in the results I had obtained in such existence.

If I had known about it earlier, I would have being more intent on making sure that each day counted; for sure I would have only focused on the successful results I wanted to accomplish and the apologies would have been extricated from my heart.

Surrendered to the will of my inner self, I made myself ready to enter into this place that, without a doubt, would show me the rhyme and reason for many of the things which went on during my life. Among many of my questions, I wondered why I had to live such a life, why die in such a way, why did I have to go through so many obstacles to get what I wanted, why those parent, why did I wish to learn certain things and not others, etc.

To go through that place would bring me clarity and understanding, so the time had come.

PART IV

KNOWLEDGE

"I want to know His thoughts, the rest are details."

Albert Einstein

To pretend to use words in order to describe a new and ineffable place where the lessons would take place would be rude and grotesque. The only word I can think could come close to describe it is 'perfection.' The sounds, the light, the atmosphere, the temperature, the smells, the landscape; everything was a synonym for perfection.

At the front door of the first cloister, there was a sign illuminating the entrance; up above, well centered, in golden, capital letters that seemed to be gold plated, and it read the following:

FIRST RUNE
GOD

- God is in everything, unlimited and infinite, without beginning or end; omnipresent because he is in every place; omniscient because he knows it all; omnipotent because he can do everything.
- You are in God; as such, it is inaccurate to consider that God is in you.
- You will never be able to separate from God because He is all, and you are part of that whole. No matter what you do, you will never be able to separate from God.
- You are a spiritual creature living and experiencing the material.
- Given that God is all, nothing is outside of Him; so, the devil is that human part that leads you to the unwanted results.
- You were created in the same image of God, because of that, you are powerful, unlimited and wise. Each one of your atoms belongs to God and each atom of God belongs to you. You are one with all there is; what limits you is ignorance, the same one that prevents you from realizing your own divinity.
- The All follows a certain set of immutable laws which work, whether you know them or not, and the happiness of human beings is directly related to their level of knowledge and alignment with such laws.
- You and any other person are equal; the only difference between you and them is the results you

get; and if you want to, you could obtain the same results.
- The good and the bad are relative to the eyes of the beholder. Human beings do not see the world as it is, rather as they are.
- Because God is all and you are in God, both truth and lie inhabit all of your being, and so do kindness, evil, justice and injustice. All the opposites inhabit your being, and you can choose to live in the light or under the guise of your own shadow.
- In essence, all atoms which compose nature are equal, and the only thing that changes is the distance between them and the speed at which they move; as such, all animate or in–animate beings share the same essence, regardless of the kingdom to which they belong.
- Limits do not exist, they are self–imposed because of your ignorance of what you really are: an unlimited being, filled with power, wisdom and love.
- For you, everything is possible, even becoming what you are not yet.

YOU AND GOD ARE A UNIT.
AS SUCH,
RECOGNIZE YOUR DIVINITY

TEST TO CONFIRM YOU HAVE LEARNED THE LESSON:

- ❖ Look for the face of God in every person.

- ❖ When in doubt, call for God's rightful guidance. The way to do it is by simply calling Him from your heart so that only the greatest good permeates your life.

- ❖ Feel you are united with Him on a continuous basis, and recognize that it is impossible to separate from Him regardless of what you do, or where you are.

When I reflected upon this test, I realized that even though it seemed to be very simple, it was not something I constantly practiced.

Despite how logical and simple the words on the rune sounded, I refused to believe that everything could be that way. However, every time I read the words I found they had a new sense, and I was able to achieve a greater level of acceptance. As I accepted them, I recognized that up until that point in my life I had been mistaken. I went over all my beliefs regarding God. Since I was a boy, I was educated to fear God, the image of a punishing God who kept putting me to the test and only existed in the good things, because Satan lived in the bad things and God always went away from him and anybody who misbehaved. So now, it turns out that it is impossible to be apart from God because He is everything. No matter what I do, or where I am, I am always in God. Maybe this separation, which is either mental or imaginary, has been the cause of so many problems, many wars and lacks, and the cause of much suffering and sickness. This is the time to recognize the truth, for not in vain where these words said to us long ago: "The truth will set you free."

It really caught my attention; I understood and accepted that all that power had always been in me, and because of my level of ignorance up to that moment, I had not been able to recognize it and make use of it.

There was a surge of questions coming from my heart and I wanted to meet again with my Guardian Angel, with that part of God which belongs to me, that guides me and to which I belong. I was waiting for him to answer many of those questions, although now I was all alone, like in a state of introspection, with a clear consciousness and lucid about many things.

Could this place be what many called paradise? The sound of the wind was like a sweet melody and the temperature was perfect. In the distance, I could see a majestic, multicolored garden, and there He was. I did not know anymore whether I should call him God or Guardian Angel. I could not find the word to name Him.

"What have you learned?" He asked me.

"I must confess that I am very confused." I said. *"If God is everything, then who are you? Many people wait to die in order to meet their creator, and all they sacrifice in life makes no sense, for it would be enough to just go and do as we please without thinking about the consequences."*

More than in time, we moved in space toward parallel worlds, to that initial place where we go back to when death comes to us. I observed the new comers, the ones who had just died. I was surprised to see how each one of them encountered their own Guardian Angel, their own God, in many shapes and forms. Not everyone saw Him in their own image; some of them saw Jesus Christ, others saw Buddha, Muhammad, Krishna, the Virgin Mary; others encountered images I could not recognize, I only knew they represented something sacred; others saw a multicolored, celestial light.

Then God said: *"Just as every drop of sea water contains all the elements of the sea, without being the whole sea, so you contain the totality of my essence without you being God. Just as all the drops unite in order to form the great ocean, when you love and become one with everything, you are God."*

"Who are you? And, why do you assume this form and not any other?" I asked.

"I am you, and I assume the form that your intellect gives me, just as I take on the image every person you just saw, holds of me." He replied. *"Those who do not project a preconceived form see the light, because in essence we are light."*

"If we are one, why did you wait until now to speak to me?" I asked Him.

"Since always, and at all times, I have spoken to you in many languages and in multiple ways. Sometimes I was the voice of your consciousness; other times I was your intuition or common sense. Many times I communicated with signals or coincidences, but you refused to listen and trust me." He said.

⚜

Again, I fell into a state of silence and introspection. Inside of me, the voice of my consciousness, the Sacred Angel, told me that – for the moment – this information was enough and it was time to continue with my journey.

Something in me knew that later on we would go into the subject of doing and undoing; so I continued with the journey, and further along I was able to see the second cloister with its bright sign hanging on the door.

SECOND RUNE
PURPOSES AND DREAMS

- Every human being is born with a purpose which resides within their hearts; the journey of life is to discover it and put it to the service of humanity.
- Your personal story is written in the book of life; you had a lifespan that allowed you to tread the path of your own story, which is conceived with the idea of getting you ever closer to your own divinity.
- When the person cannot find the purpose of his life, the tendency is to live in vice.
- When you are following your purpose, there is fullness and happiness in your life. When you find yourself trapped by the slavery of vice, you create false moments of ecstasy that, inevitably, bring you moments of sadness, depression and loneliness.
- The important thing in the journey of life is the person you become when you follow your path in the search for the realization of your dreams.
- A being is only as big as the dreams he dares to live.
- In the conquering of a new dream, your own being requires new qualities. If you turn into the person who deserves to have such a dream come true, all of your limitations will disappear.
- To live with purpose or in vice is the dilemma we are confronted with at every single moment. The purpose keeps us alive, fills us with illusions and hopes. The vice traps you and leads you to death.
- If you focus on your dreams and reach for your inner strength, everything will be possible in the world.

- The heart's dreams are for the greater good and the highest goals. The dreams of the ego are only for the benefit of the individual.
- Your heart's dreams make you feel united with God; they unite you with His unlimited power. The dreams of the ego make you feel separated, alone and incapable; they turn you into a competitive being and make you forget that the only being you need to compete against is yourself.
- To dream is one of the keys to happiness. Dreams are the elixir of eternal youth.
- Who gives you hope, gives you life; who steals your hopes or destroys your ideas, annihilates you. As such, choose well who you share with.
- You only begin to age and die when you stop dreaming. The greatest dreamers of all times are more alive today than ever.
- Every dream that comes from your heart has been placed there by God, because He knows you have the power to materialize it.
- Do not skip any dream. Dreams give you the best chance to discover your unlimited power.
- A man who dreams while sleeping is harmless; the one who dreams awake is powerful, his dreams can be either a curse or a blessing; it can work toward the destruction or the construction of a better world.
- Even more important than dreaming big is the length of time a person has the courage to continue to dream big.
- Utilize your gifts; they have been given to you by God as a means to serve your kin. Follow your heart's dreams and you will discover the purpose of your life.
- Big dreams call for big actions; small dreams call for small actions. Dreams without actions are just an illusion.

- Dream the impossible and the possible will easily come true.
- Human history only remembers those great dreamers who went beyond the paradigms of what was considered to be realistic by those who thought their dreams were impossible.
- Dreamer or realistic? It is your choice: as a dreamer, you are free and unlimited; as a realistic, you are trapped in the past and within the boundaries of your imaginary limits.

TEST TO CONFIRM YOU HAVE LEARNED THE LESSON:

- ❖ Write down all of your dreams without judging any of them and read them frequently in order to derive strength, hope and the desire to live.

- ❖ Count all your gifts; write them down on a list and clearly define in which way you would like to apply them in the service of humanity.

- ❖ Place your gifts and your dreams in the hands of God so that all of your creations will be always made for the greater good.

At the end of this cloister – with an even brighter light – I could read the following words:

EVERYTHING STARTS WITH A DREAM

And they continued to resonate within my mind. How can I accept that everything starts with a dream? Had I not told myself, over and over, I had to be realistic? Words like: "Do not be unrealistic," "Get down from that cloud." My best friends expressed these phrases in their attempts to keep me from suffering pain or a great disappointment. As soon as some new idea emerged from my heart, I would immediately find some opponents to it; most of the times these people would have thousands of arguments to justify why they thought my idea would never work. In very few occasions did I find someone who actually encouraged me and even gave me ideas on how to make my dreams come true; they did not mean to be evil, they just did not want to see me suffering.

If the key to happiness is to dream – meaning, to have hope and find a greater meaning to life – then poverty, suffering and violence happen to the degree that more and more people stop dreaming. As such, it is urgent to get more individuals involved on this task, and become angels of hope, creators, and motivate people to dream.

To kill someone else's dream should be considered a crime, because it destroys the real purpose of life: to regain our power.

As I pondered about this, I remembered those moments in the past when I had undermined my own abilities, or told myself that something was not possible; even worse, in the midst of my supreme ignorance, many times I told others what they could or could not possibly accomplish. Had I been more informed, I would have dedicated my life to inspire others, to cheer them up and encourage them to pursue each one of their dreams and focus on accomplishing them. For sure, this is what Walt Disney meant when he said: "Beware of those who poison wells, those people who go around the world telling each new idea that it is not possible," to which I would add: because they are the breeders of unhappiness on Earth.

Life is a bundle of dreams to be fulfilled. From the moment we are born, and throughout or childhood, we dream about many things without care for limitations until the 'realistic' adults begin to point out what, according to them, is or is not possible. It is in the nature of children to dream, which is the reason they are such happy beings. We are all born equipped to be happy and enjoy life while we discover our unlimited power and recognize our unity with God. Now I understand the parable of the talents.

What would it be like if life was like a great orchestra that has to play a symphony, and just because they did not play my instrument as they should have, I robbed the others of the opportunity to enjoy the whole melody? I had a quick reflection on the matter: those who cannot find their purpose in life and put it to the service of humanity, are also robbing others. I deduced that to find one's purpose in life is as simple as closing your eyes, focus your attention on the beat of your heart and ask for guidance, with the certainty that the ultimate truth will emerge from it. Shakespeare used to say: "Go within; summon your heart and ask it what you do not know." I wondered what the purpose of my life could be.

My self–growth and spiritual development instructor used to say the following: "The heart holds all of the answers to our questions. However, few people go looking for answers in their hearts. We need to go back to the heart, over and over again because whatever comes from there comes from God, and God has the best answers for each one of us."

I was assailed by a stinging feeling: "If only I would have done it," I understood I could only aspire to learn these lessons which, as always, came late into my life. A warm breeze blew toward me and brought me out of that introspection, and I recognized the presence of the sacred part of me.

"You must get the most important part of the message: dreams are the wishes God holds for you, and to materialize them is to do the Will of the Divine. Ahh! All dreams are sacred, no matter how absurd or impossible they seem; and do not worry, because all of these will be imprinted in your memory for all eternity; if you were to be born again – as many do – you would be a great dreamer, capable of transforming the history humanity.

To say things like 'If I was born again' is just as absurd as if you said to me, 'if you would go back to sleep and dreamed about the same thing, do not forget...' There is no point in saying 'could have', 'should have'... What happened in the past has already happened, and given the opportunity, we can only learn from it in order to avoid repeating what we do not like.

"Now you understand that everything on Earth has a purpose, and the life of those who do not determine theirs has no meaning. It is as if you went on a trip and all of a sudden you suffer from amnesia, and you forget where you are going and from where you come; and so, if you went south, then west, east and then north, and then continue to go on without knowing why or what for, then the only thing which would give meaning to the moment would be the experience of an emotion or something that brings excitement into your life. Just like that, people who have not found the purpose of their life fall prey to vice as a result of their lack of direction, or in order to leave the monotony of their every day. Nonetheless, human beings carry within their hearts a purpose to better the world; to find this purpose is the first reason for human existence, and to put it to the service of humanity is the meaning of life. Many times people get lost in life and need a good shake up in order to orient themselves; for example, some people create accidents without understanding that the purpose of their lives is hidden in their dreams, so close to them they cannot see it. In order to see it, it is necessary to go within yourself, to the light of your heart, to which Jesus the Christ referred to when he said: 'I am the way, the truth and the life.' The words 'I AM' are the keywords which have always been utilized in order to manifest the light that everyone carries within themselves, and to connect with their unlimited power, meaning, to connect you and I, and be one in the light."

I replied to Him the following: *"If choosing between living in purpose or living in vice is such a simple thing to do – or so it appears –, then why so many people get trapped in the illusion of some vice like alcohol, drugs, food, sex, TV, and even work, just to run away from themselves? I must assume that to live one's purpose means to love what one does, but that is not a common thing; if I think about it well, I believe there is more people living in vice than living in purpose."*

To which he responded: *"Many stop believing in their dreams and looking for internal guidance. In some cases, either through religious exposure or as a result of some fortuitous event, a person may experience a state of unity with God, and the meaning of life resurfaces and turns them into beings that profess their beliefs through their religions, and they may come to think that this is the only way to achieve it, the only one with value. In many cases, they turn into fanatics that love a God who lacks creativity to guide His children toward their own personal story. You, yourself, may now find the main reason and the why of so many people who live in vice: their non–existent state of separation from God."*

I went into a deep silence, into a deep contemplation; I could only perceive the murmur of the wind and the nuances of that beautiful place. I felt connected with the nothing, and I felt these moments filled me with eternity. Unfortunately, this was a source of contradicting emotions; I felt gratitude for being able to understand so many things, yet at the same time I felt frustration, to imagine how different my life could have been if I had received this information at an earlier point in time. I felt as if someone was testing or evaluating me for something I had not being prepared for, and I felt it was not fair I should take the test first and then receive the lesson. I was confused; however, I intuitively knew that very soon I would receive some answers to my conundrum. I walked in silence, living the experience of being a part of everything.

In the distance, I saw what I assumed was the next subject to learn.

THIRD RUNE
THE LAW OF RANG: EVERYTHING IS POSSIBLE

- Everything is possible. Most of the things which are possible today were just a mere illusion in the past, something farfetched from reality.
- Limits only exist for those who accept them. The human being determines the parameters of what is possible or impossible. The contribution to humanity from those who have made history is to have stretched the limits of what was possible, to have achieved something that in their time was considered impossible by others.
- Whether you believe you can, or you cannot, you are right.
- Faith and fear are the two opposite poles of certainty; both tend to materialize.
- Certainty allows for anything to become possible.
- Limits are self–imposed; break them and you will make history.
- Every person determines the time needed to make something possible; it could be right now, or it may take a century.
- Doubt arises due to lack of proper information, and it ends up by destroying your creations.
- Eliminate the word 'impossible' from your vocabulary; just say: For now, I do not know how to do it.
- It is your choice whether to obtain information, knowledge, wisdom and certainty, or to live in disinformation, ignorance, folly and doubt.

- Choose who you share with: with the magi of the possible, who know they are unlimited and find that God is the source of their power and supreme wisdom; or those who believe that every new idea is impossible and create limits for you.
- In God, everything is possible for everyone, and in Him, limits do not exist. In the ego you are limited, and it leads you to compete with others because you are always thinking about defeating or being defeated, as well as the fact that some people win while others lose.
- Your beliefs tilt the balance in one way or the other, making you choose between "the kingdom and a plate of beans."

TEST TO CONFIRM YOU HAVE LEARNED THE LESSON:

- ❖ Eliminate the following phrases from your vocabulary: 'I cannot,' 'impossible,' or 'I do not know.' Instead, replace them for expressions which manifest the relativity of the moment, such as: 'For now, I do not know how to do it,' 'at this precise moment, I do not have the necessary information to execute this,' or 'it is highly improbable I will be able to do it right this moment.'

I burst out laughing, forgetting I was in a sacred place and other people were present during the lesson with me; I did not care. I thought that given the fact this world was so perfect, maybe nobody actually heard me, even though it appeared as if my voice resounded in this place with a pounding force which could only be compared with what would come out of some special effects study in Hollywood. 'The kingdom and a plate of beans?' I was laughing inside for having made such a basic mistake, and for not having understood the depth of this most logical affirmation. In life, whether by lack of certainty or holding the wrong kind of beliefs, my ego took pride in what I was capable of doing or having, yet my self–esteem would break down every time I observed my results in the solitude of my private moments. What a pity! Now everything seems so simple, and to think that in those times I unconsciously chose the plate of beans rather than the kingdom, which belongs to me by divine right.

The phrase 'everything is possible' resounded inside my head repeatedly, like a buzzing, especially because it was so easy to say it, but so hard to live it. Now it turns out that limits are self–imposed and everything responds to our level of certainty. According to these teachings given by my Sacred Being, the doubt – most faithful companion – which in life turned me into a realistic person, became a ghost I simply should have never allowed in.

"Many times when I felt dubious, I realized later on that it was something which was not good for me; so doubt is not always a negative thing." I replied to Him, feeling sure it was not as He made it sound.

This greater, all–knowing part of me smiled without judgment, filled with understanding, acceptance, patience and happiness for me. It seemed as if He took delight in my lack of conformity. I was discovering something important, and even though I could not understand much of His attitude, I liked it and it allowed me to be authentic.

"It is easy to mistake doubt with discernment." He said. *"But they are very different. You doubt something because you lack enough information, or because you are afraid of the consequences in the future; you discern when, having the right information, you choose what is best for you. You intuitively know what the right choice is when you*

are willing to listen to that part of you who knows it all; other times you may feel a hunch, or a sense of knowingness which indicates the right path. In the sense of knowingness, more than doubt, there is a certainty about the right path to choose because the information that comes from your heart has to do with your divine plan."

"And how do I know it is not an affirmation from the ego, to say that I can do it all?" I asked.

"Very simple," he responded. *"If you say 'I am capable of everything in God who makes me strong,' then your creations will materialize without pride, contempt or any other negative emotion; in turn, when you are acting from your ego you feel the need to fight and compete, and those achievements are filled with pitfalls and difficulties."*

I saw no purpose in asking questions, for it seemed everything had such an obvious explanation that I felt clumsy for not been able to get it before hand. To revel in all of these questioning gave me a sense of fullness, and at moments I felt alive, meaning, as if I was living a continuation of what I used to call life; I knew that in this episode of my existence I felt more conscious than ever.

I began to wander in the infinite, living a sensation of freedom and understanding I had never had. My mind was filled with old memories, but the experience itself was fairly new to be considered unique. I felt like I wanted to laugh, scream, run, cry, jump...in short, I felt many simultaneous and conflicting emotions. I was living in perfect time; I would chose the moments and the appropriate one would come up, just as my decisions appeared to be in synchronicity with the universe, or maybe the universe was in synchronicity, and I was in it.

FOURTH RUNE
THE POWER OF THOUGHT

- The mind is powerful.
- You are the result of your predominant thoughts.
- Control your thoughts and your will control your destiny.
- To think is to create.
- Your thoughts are the result of the information you receive and the information that you constantly capture via your five senses.
- Control the information you receive and you will control your thoughts.
- You make your world into a paradise or a hell; it all depends on the kind of thoughts you are holding on your mind.
- By being responsible for the thoughts on your mind, you are being responsible for your destiny.
- Do not underestimate the power of every thought. Make sure that what you are thinking is exactly what you want in life.
- Concentrate only in what you want in life, and that which you do not desire will disappear from your reality.
- Whenever you are imagining, meaning, whenever you are creating something, pay close attention to colors, brightness, size, texture, sounds, volume, temperature, distance, and any other detail of the image; to remember feelings of fullness, trust, happiness and security are a sure sign you are in the

right path of your creation. Do not disregard the details; they make a great deal of difference.
- The information you receive gives you knowledge, which generates your beliefs; your beliefs generate your attitudes; your attitude conditions your actions; your repetitive actions generate your habits and these lead you to obtain the results you get in life.
- The way to approach any human creation is to determine clearly what is wanted, defined in the present "eternal moment," and to receive only the information that gives us the necessary knowledge and makes us declare that what we want is possible.
- Your mind receives constant input via your senses; what you see, hear, touch, taste and smell, all of that information is the makeup of your convictions, which in turn conditions your attitude and invites you to take certain actions. The repetition of such actions creates your habits, and because of that, leads to the results you get in life.
- The conscious mind is designed to determine clear objectives. The unconscious mind is designed to generate the strategy to accomplish those objectives, and your subconscious mind has the record of the limitations you have created for yourself.
- Your mission is to define clearly the successful result which you desire for everything that you want.
- Imagine, clearly and on a constant basis, the successful result of what you want, and the universe will support you, unconditionally, to make it come true.

TEST TO CONFIRM YOU HAVE LEARNED THE LESSON:

- ❖ Practice daily visualization of what you desire to obtain in life; visualize only the successful result, and in order to obtain it place your trust in the hands of nature.

- ❖ Recognize that when you clearly know what you want, the universe takes care of all the details.

- ❖ Live the feelings which pertain and are inherent to the accomplishment of what you want, such as security, happiness, fullness or trust, and keep your creations to yourself, even after they have materialized, in order to avoid spiritual pride.

In life, and for a long time, I had studied this subject. I knew its meaning, and even though I did not get the results I wanted, it was clear I had created them as a result of my thoughts.

At some point, the self-knowledge instructor had mentioned that the mind remains in a dimension of eternity – just as my current experience demonstrated – which only means the mind is with us way before we are born, and we will continue to have it after we die. He said the brain is made out of two hemispheres, each one with opposite functions, yet they complement each other. The left hemisphere of the brain controls the right side of the body, and some of its functions are to set goals and objectives. The right hemisphere of the brain controls the left side of the body, the feminine, our creativity. I also learned we have two types of neurons called 'dwarves' by the instructor, of which some act as an archive for everything we perceive through our five senses, while others execute whatever the archivist dwarves save. For this reason, he always remarked on how important it was to pay attention to what we listened to, read or watched. He invited us to read inspiring books and works that would afford us a greater comprehension of our own power in order to attain anything we wished for, to reach anything that we set out to and to have the quality of life we desired.

On the other hand, he insisted on the idea that we should maintain a full color, mental projection of a movie in which everything we desire flows and is portrayed as if we have already achieved it; and he assured us that the universe would take care of making our wishes come true for as long as we have a clear picture of what we want. He said, for example, that one of the traits of a successful person is that they know exactly what they want, and they do daily visualizations of a movie in which they feel, hear and see themselves as the main character. I marveled many times at how my wishes would come true through the application of the visualization technique, focusing on the desired outcome, not the process of it. Yet my self–esteem would diminish as soon as I realized that what stood in the way of my accomplishing more success was my laziness to visualize what I wanted, along with the ever–present excuse that I had to leave things for later.

I thought about calling God or my Guardian Angel, but I restrained myself. Every time I understood with greater clarity that the answers He gave me, I already knew. So then, I promised myself I would go through several runes without talking to Him.

I could see the glowing sign, which identified the next cloister.

FIFTH RUNE
THE POWER OF THE WORD

- In the beginning was the Verb, and the Verb was in God and the Verb was God.
- Through Him all things were made, and without Him nothing was made that has been made.
- In Him was life, and the life was the light of men.
- Everything was created by the verb in the seven days of creation and God said:
  - Let there be light, and there was light, and the light was called 'day' and the darkness 'night.'
  - Let there be a firmament in the midst of the waters, and let it divide the waters from the waters. And God called the firmament 'Heaven.'
  - Let the water under the sky be gathered to one place, and let dry ground appear. And it was so. God called the dry ground 'land,' and the gathered waters he called 'seas.' Let he land produce vegetation: seed bearing plants and trees on the land that bear fruit with seed in it, according to their various kinds. And it was so.
  - Let there be lights in the vault of the sky to separate the day from the nights, and let them serve as signs and for seasons, and days and years. And let them be for lights in the firmament of the heaven to give light upon the earth. And it was so.

- Let the water teem with living creatures, and let birds fly above the earth across the vault of the sea. God blessed them and said: "Be fruitful and increase in number and fill the water in the seas, and let the birds increase on the earth."
- Let the land produce living creatures according to their kinds: the livestock, the creatures that move along the ground, and the wild animals, each according to its kind. And so it was.
- Let us make mankind in our image, in our likeness, so that they may rule over the fish in the sea and the birds in the sky, over the livestock and all the wild animals, and over all the creatures that move along the ground.

He blessed the seventh day and made it sacred; such was the origin of the heavens and the earth when they were made.

- Your words have power; they are seeds that create your reality.
- Affirm only what you wish to perpetuate. If you declare what you do not want, it will continue to materialize in your life.
- You are the prophet of your own life; your words are prophecies that come to pass.
- Value your word; honor your commitments and you will have a greater sense of self-esteem and self-worth.
- Words are thoughts turned into sound.
- Anything you desire you can achieve if you say it aloud, in the present tense, as a first person affirmation.

- Give thanks for what you ask, as if it has already materialized.
- Heaven and earth will pass, but your words will not.
- Be wise when using the power of your words.
- A prayer is a sentence spoken from the heart.
- To pray is to repeat a prayer.
- A prayer is the highest level, an efficient and sublime way of creating with words.
- A person who sings is praying twice.
- Mantras are words or vibratory frequencies which, as we repeat them, connect us with various levels of energy.
- There are mantras that connect you with light, while others connect you with the darkness.
- You are responsible for the mantras you repeat, whether you do it at the mental level or aloud.
- Mantras are handed down from teacher to disciple once the latter is ready for it.
- Choose to receive guidance from teachers who have proven results, worthy of what they preach.

TEST TO CONFIRM YOU HAVE LEARNED THE LESSON:

- ❖ Listen carefully to your words and choose not to be right. As soon as you hear yourself saying something which would lead to a result that is different from what you wish, say the following words out loud: "I cancel what I have just said," or "I erase what I have just said" with the purpose of preventing the materialization of this new creation.

I remember my life drastically changed the day I read a book that spoke about the power of the verb. In the book – which was given to me as a gift – it was assured that all human beings are capable of creating whatever we desire to have in the reality of our world. If two people were to repeat two completely opposite phrases every morning, for example, if you were to say: "Today is the best day o my life, I deserve only the best and I accept it now; in my life all is prosperity;" and then, at the same time of the day I say the following: "Today is a boring day, everything is expensive, I do not get anything right, money is never enough," and then we were to compare the results at the end of the day, you would realize we both were right, and that each one of us got the results which matched our own specific decrees. The author of the book challenged us to repeat our wishes in the first person, as an affirmation and in the present tense; he said that if we did this a thousand times during the day, for a lapse of forty days, no matter what we wished for, that we would be able to materialize effectively such wish. He defied us not to believe in him, and to put it to the test and then watch the results we would obtain.

Around that time, I began to repeat the following: "I «first person» am «present and affirmative» an excellent commercial announcer," and as an act of magic, I began to be hired to record commercials. Yes, it appeared as if the magi within had awakened so that my wishes would come true just as I wanted them. Every morning when I got up and had no money in my pockets, I repeated over and over the following words: "I am connected with the richness of the universe, money flows to me in abundance, legally, constantly and easily." Again, job proposals would come up out of nowhere, and money came to me with ease. Later on I got involved with a sales department and I did the same: I said to myself, "I am the best salesman in the store and I fulfill over 200% of my quota." And it so happened that way. I won several prices and I managed to work fewer hours than my co-workers because I was more efficient with my time;

everything that needed to happen in order for me to have a successful sale would just happen; the right person would show up, at the right moment and at the right place.

I knew that if a person can perceive the power of his words, recognize that everything he says comes to pass, watch for his unconscious creations and perform some verbal hygiene, then this person would be able to turn his life around marvelously, and he would know that he alone is responsible for the results.

Again, everything seemed so easy, then why is it that people are not aware they can do such a simple thing? I realized not everyone is ready to receive certain knowledge at the same time, and that knowledge, just as power and wisdom, is discovered a little at a time and when we are ready to understand it; this can only be achieved in the same measure we can heal ourselves from the heart, with love.

The wind that caressed my face allowed me to perceive the delicious smells of nature and listen to the sounds of the most beautiful music I had ever heard; the birds were singing as if in celebration of the mere fact they existed. To exist? So then, before falling into another state of introspection, I found myself standing in front of the next cloister's door.

SIXTH RUNE
THE POWER OF ACTION

- Only practiced knowledge persists in the spirit.
- Repetitive actions create habits.
- The longest walk begins with a step.
- True power lies in microscopic changes; small, repetitive actions create destiny.
- Action is the key to all human realization.
- Action cures fear.
- The moment of power is the present; begin to act now.
- The power is within you; start acting and put your power to the service of humanity.
- A real decision is followed by action.
- If you wish to get different results, do something different; if you continue doing the same, you will continue to get the same results.
- Make sure that every action you take will lead you to the result you desire.
- To postpone the action for tomorrow is to betray your dreams, and as such, yourself; this is the reason actions must be taken now and not at some other time, right at this place and not anywhere else.
- The difference between a dreamer and a self-deluded person lies in the former's capacity to act.
- Life is a game where you set goals for yourself; the obstacles arise in relationship to your goals; the bigger the goal, the bigger the obstacle; you either conquer the obstacle and succeed, or renounce your goal and fail. It is your choice. Choose to act.
- Life is a movement. When you stop acting, you begin to die.

- To expect to harvest fruits which are different from the seeds you have sown is ignorant.
- The winner is the one who keeps trying until the end.

TEST TO CONFIRM YOU HAVE LEARNED THE LESSON:

❖ Do anything you have pending on your to–do list immediately, because the unfinished business drains you of your energy and completing it augments it.

It was absolutely clear: Action is the 'abracadabra' that makes magic start flowing into our lives. I never thought – me, who used to leave everything for the next day – that the next day would never come. I would promise myself today I would for sure take action tomorrow, but the next day I would come up with a better excuse in order to keep postponing my decisions. That 'tomorrow' never came. Now I understood how late it was.

At this stage of my learning, I did not even know whether all of this information would serve a purpose. I left the cloister, and in my mind, the following phrase kept repeating itself: "action, here and now, and then magic will happen." Although my feelings were as those experienced by a student who remembers the correct answer after he has submitted the test, an answer which he always knew but he could not properly answer. I abandoned myself to the perfection and the happiness of not being judged.

The atmosphere I breathed made me feel at peace with myself. I decided to act, and I quickly went to the next cloister.

SEVENTH RUNE
FEELINGS AND EMOTIONS

- Feelings are the connection between body and spirit, through the senses and the mind.
- Feelings are sacred.
- To listen to your body is to listen to God.
- Your body is made out of cells that hold memory, in which the senses record all of your experiences from the moment of conception.
- Your feelings guide you to the right path and give you power.
- Your feelings arise from within you and they are projected outwardly.
- Emotions arise as a result of outer stimuli.
- There are emotions which empower you and charge you with energies, while others envelop you and take away your power, meaning, they either strengthen or weaken you.
- To differentiate between a feeling and an emotion is the direct result of human sensitivity at its highest level of expression.
- Do not judge what you feel; on the contrary, listen to yourself and you will find information which will lead you through the right path.
- Feelings of depression, boredom and disappointment are a sign that you are not in alignment with your purpose.
- Your personal transformation is directly related to the domain of the seven capital sins, in which you spend most of your energies.

TEST TO CONFIRM YOU HAVE LEARNED THE LESSON:

- ❖ Be aware of your internal, negative reactions and observe what caused such a response from within your being, this will allow you to judge when you are being trapped by an emotion.

Many times in my life, I was a prisoner of my own beliefs, and on several occasions, I refused to feel, mainly because – as I understand now – I could not distinguish between a feeling and an emotion. Feelings never lie; if one wants to sleep, for sure one is sleepy, the same if one wishes to laugh or cry. Therefore, this is what I used to do and then later on I would find myself in a state of fullness.

However, whenever I was trapped by an emotion, like jealousy, I felt weak. I had a constant, internal battle with the seven capital sins, "lust, envy, greed, laziness, gluttony, pride and wrath," but I rarely won any of these battles. The important thing was to develop the sensibility and be capable of discernment.

I walked for another while. I wandered around this paradise in a conscious state of presence I had never experienced before. I also felt tired, saturated; the same sensation experienced when one intensifies the study of a subject of special interest. I wanted to stop all the learning and just enjoy, which at the same time made me feel remorseful. I wanted to stop all the mental chatter, even though I knew it was not possible at the moment, and the best thing to do would be to accept what was going on and abandon myself to the experience, specially because some higher part of me knew that everything was temporary, and even this stage would also come to an end. Hence, the best thing I could do was to enjoy it. Once again, I heard the sacred part of me and I felt relieved.

"How do you feel?" He asked.

"Even more confused than before" I answered.

"Little by little you will make sense of these lessons, and you will know the 'why' and 'what for' of each one of them." He said.

I knew this puzzle had many pieces, but for now I was only able to see some of them; I would have preferred to see the whole game and the part corresponding to my own evolution, with the purpose of understanding the rhyme and reason of this experience.

EIGHTH RUNE
THE NOURISHMENT

- The body is nourished by what you eat, by feelings and every breath you take.
- When you nourish your body, make sure you are giving it nutrients and not poison.
- Nourishment, or food, can be alkaline, neutral or acidic.
- Alkaline foods are those whose pH is higher than seven, such as beef, fish, eggs, salts and some green vegetables. These foods contract your body, they are in charge of creating and maintaining your bone and muscular structure, and they have the ability to keep your consciousness focused on the past.
- Neutral foods are all the cereals. They are in charge of proper nourishment of your blood system and they have the ability to keep your consciousness focused on the present.
- Acidic foods are those whose pH is lower than seven, such as flours, some vegetables, alcohol and sweets. These dilate your body, exert a powerful influence on your nervous system and have the ability to keep your consciousness focused on the future.
- In a world where everything is relative, you need to ingest the three kinds of foods and handle the concepts of the main and the secondary. Mainly, you require ingesting neutral foods that allow you to stay focused on the present, and complement them with alkaline and acidic foods.

- Learn to listen to your body, and it will teach you the wisest way to nourish it.
- If you wish to live a long life, eat little and chew a lot.
- Only nourish your mind with information which empowers you and leads to the discovery of the unlimited power within the light of your heart, and then put it to the service of humanity.
- Nourishment is received via the five senses of the body.
- There are three types of nourishment: Physical, mental and spiritual.
- The physical body receives nourishment through what you eat and feel, with which you manifest either health or disease.
- There is no such thing as a perfect diet. Each human being is capable of determining what is adequate in his case depending on, among other things, the work he performs, age, the place where he lives and his physical constitution.
- The mind is nourished with the information that you receive via your five senses, which in turn generates your beliefs.
- The spirit is nourished by every breath you take, by focusing your attention on the absolute and the eternal through prayer, contemplation, spiritual disciplines and meditation.
- To meditate is to listen to the sacred voice of God. To practice a spiritual discipline is to walk constantly toward the light of God. To contemplate is to delight in the light of God and to pray is to speak to God.

TEST TO CONFIRM YOU HAVE LEARNED THE LESSON:

- ❖ Eat little and chew a lot.

- ❖ Be alert; select the information that you obtain via the five senses.

- ❖ Remain in constant communication with God.

If we were fair, we should focus daily on nourishing our physical, mental and spiritual aspects in a manner which is correct and equal. In turn, we constantly feed – in a bad way – our physical and mental bodies, and we only think about our spirit in times of need or crisis. Maybe the body remains trapped because of our vices, and as such, our mind and spirit cannot feed correctly. I remembered the phrase, "a healthy mind in a healthy body," and with it the analogy of the horse and the rider; our body is the horse, our mind is the rider and the wonderful race of life is only won by the one whose horse and rider are both healthy.

I continued in silence, not allowing myself to engage any further internal dialogues. I only wanted to feel; to live. I observed as my feet joined the floor beneath me. After a while though, I looked up and saw the sign with the name of my next lesson.

NINTH RUNE
THE BREATH

- Your cells are programmed by each breath and through your feelings, which is later reflected in your energy field in order for you to attract, with the force of a powerful magnet, what has been recorded there.
- The ether, a substance that encompasses everything, the origin of eternity, contains all the qualities of God; when you breathe it in you can obtain from Him everything which you desire in life: health or sickness, prosperity or lack, love or hate, light or darkness.
- When you breathe in through your nose, you feed your spirit; when you breathe in through your mouth, you connect with your lower energy centers.
- When you wish for something, you need only breathe it in and feel how you attract it from the ether, and then record it in your cells.
- Do not underestimate the power of the breath. Breathe in deeply and the blessings in your life will be evident.
- Breathe in deeply every happy moment of your life, so they will keep repeating over and over again.
- Whenever you have a question or some internal dilemma, become conscious of your breathing and the answers will arise from within you.
- Sensitivity, the ability to perceive every aspect of your life, its worth and true meaning, increases whenever you become conscious of your breathing.

🌀 When you apply conscious breathing you become the observer, and as a result, emotions cannot get a hold of you.

TEST TO CONFIRM YOU HAVE LEARNED THE LESSON:

❖ Remain conscious of your breathing and turn every inhalation into a sigh.

At some point in my life I heard that some religious leaders invite people to dedicate a part of their free time to breathe in the quality or virtue which they are lacking, and to bring it into their lives. Same thing can be done with each of the things we wish for. I even knew how important it was to be mindful of the events that happen around us when we breathe, we should make sure we only breathe in things which are pleasing, because when we breathe, we program the attraction toward ourselves of all of those emotions going around us. Besides, I knew from experience that by just altering the rhythms and cycles of my breath it is possible to connect with my cellular memory, and with it, I can bring to the present memories from the past which have been long forgotten by my conscious mind.

As I made my way to the next cloister, I pondered about all the power I could have had in life just by making use of my breathing in order to release my emotions, to not fall prey to them, and as a result, avoid so much energy loss. Just by breathing correctly, I would have been able to program myself for success, happiness, living a full life and materialize my wishes.

TENTH RUNE
SILENCE

- You need to silence your mind in order to listen to your body and connect with what you feel. In this way, and through your senses, your body will give you valuable information, a feedback which will indicate to you the most appropriate way to treat what your body is telling you.
- You need to silence your mind in order to listen to your spirit and connect with the flow of God's sound. This will allow you to communicate with the creating source of everything and obtain answers to your most important questions.
- Just as fasting from food regenerates and heals your body, so fasting from information recharges your physical, mental and spiritual energy. Disconnect from the radio, television, newspapers and general reading in order to stay in silence and enjoy being in contact with yourself; nature and light will lead you to live more fully in the present.
- Dedicate sometime of your day to be in silence and the enjoyment of just being.
- Dedicate one day of your year to be in silence. For every day of silence, you will add another day of life and youth to your life.
- Many people hide their incapacity to feel in excessive, compulsive chatter.
- When you remain in silence, you turn into the observer and it pulls you out of senseless dialogues that make you fall into competition.

- To listen is a gift that is acquired with the ability to be silent.
- Remain silent unless what you are going to say is absolutely necessary and will elevate the other participants in the dialogue.
- Just as being silent turns into an ability not to participate in the mundane chatter, the ability to silence your internal dialogues will give you the faculty to listen to the voice of your consciousness.
- To meditate is to listen to God and the way to achieve this communication is through silence.
- You learn from listening, not from talking.
- You received two ears and one mouth so you can listen double of what you speak.

TEST TO CONFIRM YOU HAVE LEARNED THE LESSON:

> ❖ Dedicate one day of each year to live the experience of being in silence. Do not speak to anybody, do not listen to the radio, do not watch the television, do not read; this means, only your five senses experiencing the eternal present.

At one point in my life, I tried to do a verbal fast; it was very difficult. More than once, toward noon and in an unconscious manner, I either spoke to someone or spoke to myself as if words were spilling out of everywhere. I remember going on a food fast several times, sometimes for even longer than just a day and I had no issue other than the initial hunger that one experiences followed by the happiness of the sensation of having conquered something. Verbal fast, which consist on no talking, no radio, no television, no reading, just feeling, now that was something highly intense.

Those are higher realms of knowledge, I thought to myself, remembering how Jesus spent forty days and forty nights in complete fasting.

ELEVENTH RUNE
THE SEXUAL ENERGY

- Sexual energy is the raw material with which you make your dreams come true.
- Sexual energy is the most sacred of your energies, the end of all the best and the worse in you.
- When you share your sexuality, you either honor or dishonor yourself, which depends on who you establish a sexual relationship with.
- Sex is the way in which souls make love in the physical plane.
- You have auras or energy fields that surround you. One of them reflects your physical state, your levels of health or sickness. Another one, a bigger one, reflects everything that you think and speak about; it creates what is commonly known as good or bad luck. A third one expresses your level of evolution, where your forty–eight seals or runes are recorded, meaning, your life's purpose. All energy fields reflect colors, sounds and vibrations that are easily perceived by devices capable of reading these energies.
- Your auras are magnets which attract into your life what has been recorded in them; this is how you go about creating your reality in the world.

- Every time you have a sexual relationship with someone, you are mixing your auras with those of the other person, and with that, you attract either health or disease, good or bad luck, and lessons which, in some cases, you have not had or already had but now have to repeat.
- The quality of your energy changes every time you have a sexual relationship with someone.
- A man's energy diminishes every time he ejaculates.
- The wisest of humanity and the greatest of teachers had no sex during their vital cycle.
- Your attraction field and your magnetism are directly related to the amount of sexual energy that you are running.
- Sexual energy stimulates your creativity; the more sexual energy you have in your body, the greater your capacity to create from the light.
- At the moment of your death, you will need this energy in order to transition to a new learning phase, just as in life you need it in order to maneuver from sickness to health.
- When you share your sexuality you are sharing the most sacred part of you.
- Sexuality is designed to create life, equilibrium and pleasure at the inferior levels.
- Equilibrium is achieved when you acquire in yourself the virtues you desire to observe in your couple, and you transmit them through the exchange of energies – during the sexual act – in order to awaken the desire for transformation.
- When you control your sexual activity, you turn into a magnet. You must be careful; just like a light bulb that attracts many inferior insects when is turned on, when you are filled with light you will attract beings of

inferior energy, bearing emotions that rob you of your energy.
- There is a difference between controlling and suppressing your sexuality; you control it when you do not entertain sexual thoughts; you suppress it when you entertain sexual thoughts but you abstain from the sexual act.
- Sexuality is one of the last lessons you will learn, you must first master your emotions.
- When you learn everything about sexuality you will be ready for ascension or, as it may also be called, physical immortality.

TEST TO CONFIRM YOU HAVE LEARNED THE LESSON:

- ❖ Abstain from sex for a good amount of time, both physically and mentally, especially when you wish to be more creative or to create more rapidly. You will marvel at the results.

Sex always worried me. The awakenings of my sexuality lead me to discover a new level of pleasure, bursting with anxiety and attraction; I awakened to a new level of maturity and self-knowledge. At some stage in my life, in which I had already read many things about the importance of sexual energy and its proper use, I chose to go through periods of sexual abstinence and it was amazing to see how fast my wishes would materialize. Besides, the more control I had over my energy, the more conscious I became of the attraction it produced on the opposite sex.

I understand that it was – nothing more, nothing less than – the reason why the history of the greatest of humanity's teachers and thinkers of all times is so intimately related to their capacity for self-control. The history of Saint

Augustine becomes interesting from the moment he begins to take control of his sexual energy. Now, it turns out we even need this energy in order to die. It was a shame to understand that men and women who wasted their energies are people without magnetism, they have no magnet.

I wandered for a while. Not even my confused and at times darkened thoughts got in the way of my ability to feel the marvel of so much beauty. In the distance, I noticed another rune; I knew I had to continue with my learning, so I went toward it.

TWELFTH RUNE
THE FLOW OF ENERGY

- Energy flows in and from each cell in your body.
- You have several energy centers which are called seals, chakras or energy vortexes.
- The seals, chakras or energy vortexes allow for the functioning of your vital organs.
- You possess seven seals or higher chakras, ninety–two secondary ones and more than a thousand points of energetic interconnection.
- When the proper flow of energies is obstructed, pain ensues in order to let you know that something in your physical body is not being correctly used.
- When the flow of energies is adequate, your cells regenerate automatically; the opposite leads to aging and death.
- Aging, for the most part, is an unconscious choice.

- The first seal or chakra sits in the genitals area and at the base of the spinal cord, or coccyx, which is why sometimes it is also called base chakra, fundamental, muladara, sacrum or kundalini. It is associated with creativity, giving life, creating equilibrium and the will to live. At the physical level, it handles the functioning of the genital organs and sexuality.
- The second seal or navel chakra, located at the belly button is called spleen chakra; it receives and sub-divides the energy which comes from the sun. For this reason, it is known as the center of power. This chakra is the engine that propels the functioning of several important organs like the liver, pancreas, spleen and the adrenal glands. Its energy is wasted with anger, envy, pride, guilt and resentment.
- The third seal or solar plexus chakra is located below the sternum. It is considered a second brain, the center for sensitivity, the emotions, the strength and freedom to act. At the physical level, it governs the gallbladder and the nervous system.
- The fourth seal or heart chakra is located at the sternum. It is the place where the Christ energy is activated and the door to contemplation of the light of God. At the physical level, it governs the thymus, heart, blood and the circulatory system. It is the center of love.
- The fifth seal or throat chakra is located at the throat. It is the center of ambition, communication, expression, speech and hearing. At the physical level, it governs the thyroid, bronchi, lungs and the digestive tract. This is where the creative power of verb is generated.
- The sixth chakra or frontal is located in between the eyes and is known as the third eye. At the physical level, it governs the pituitary or anterior and posterior

hypophysis. It is the creative center of thought and paranormal phenomena.
- The seventh chakra or crown, known as the flower of a thousand petals, is located at the top of the head. It is the center of pure knowledge and intuition; its energy marks the evolution of every human being and connects him with his purpose in life. At the physical level, it governs the pineal gland.

TEST TO CONFIRM YOU HAVE LEARNED THE LESSON:

❖ Visualize each seal or chakra as a wheel that turns clockwise, at the speed that you consider to be perfect, radiating light that will automatically fill your vital organs with health.

Vortexes of energy I never saw... I was finally able to make sense of some information I had once received and that I simply misjudged, or did not take into consideration, such as acupuncture, which unblocks our energy centers so they can flow and improve the functioning of our vital organs. We lacked so much knowledge about ourselves that we were completely innocent of the horrible way in which we were damaging our body.

I understood that the higher the quality of our energy, the greater the chance of being trapped by emotions which make us react in such an irrational way that, in the majority of the cases, only lead us to feel regret after having already wasted our energy. Sex, I thought, and money bring a lot of inconvenience to most of the people, and they become chains from which we need to be liberated, transcend them as soon as possible. To have dominion over these two aspects of our lives was a beautiful, and at the same time hard task to do, for the person must have given the best of him in order to achieve it.

After a long and rewarding meditation, I returned to the learning path. Everything was shining with the light of the midday sun and I knew that the light that illuminated my life was no longer external; it was internal, and if I just connected with the spirit it would illuminate everything once more.

THIRTEENTH RUNE
FORGIVENESS

- To forgive is to love unconditionally.
- True forgiveness happens when a person gives thanks for the lessons learned from experiences which were riddled with resentment.
- If you can remember with affection the person who you used to resent, you will have forgiven them from your heart.
- When you go against the natural order and its laws, your tendency is to self–destruct. It is for this reason that when you hold on to the resentment which was produced by a certain situation or person, you might be unknowingly creating cancer in your body.
- You have as many debts as people or situations you resent. Forgive unconditionally and prosperity will reign in your life.
- The most important person you need to forgive is yourself. Declare yourself innocent, because anybody else in your place, with your same level of knowledge and evolution, would have acted just as you did.
- All human beings are innocent and each one acts in the best way they can, in their own way. To feel resented is of no use, for the universe is in charge of teaching us what is necessary and it will do it when the need to harvest the fruit of what we sow is most pressing. You sow innocently, and you harvest innocently; you change nothing with resentment, you only hurt yourself.

- If you declare forgiveness without forgetting, you have not forgiven.
- To forgive and to love are synonyms which invite you to live with acceptance, and acceptance is the other key to happiness.
- When you forgive others and yourself you accomplish the activation of the Christ energy within your heart, and with that, you create a sharper communication with your Creator. This is what Jesus Christ referred to when he declared: "Before attempting to enter the house of my father, you need to invoke the forgiveness of all the people you have offended and send your forgiveness to those that have offended you."
- To resent is to continue to feel something that already happened, and by doing so you stop enjoying the present.
- Resentment arises from the difference between what a person does and what you expect them to do; remember, if you were in their place you would act just as them. To accept, forgive and forget will release you from resentment.
- Guilt, that thing you do not to forgive you, produces arthritis. Free yourself from the "I should" and accept yourself unconditionally.

TEST TO CONFIRM YOU HAVE LEARNED THE LESSON:

> ❖ When you feel offended by someone, express forgiveness in your mind and in your heart. Say, "I forgive you, for you do not know what you are doing." Moreover, when you find yourself tempted to judge yourself, declare: I am the son of God, perfect, growing in grace.

As a little boy, I was taught God is the one who forgives. However, at this moment I understand that in order to live consciously in God I should have forgiven and recognized that the only option one has concerning the past is to learn from it, to transform what we do not like about it and to persist with the construction of what we like. In short, to forgive others and myself, and to accept others and myself are all necessary in order for me to connect with my own unlimited power for the greater good.

While I walked the path to the next rune, I wondered how much time had passed since that day when I first started this process.

FOURTEENTH RUNE
CREATIVITY

- Creativity is infinite.
- There is always an easier and better way to do things.
- Creativity is the antidote against all poverty.
- To create is to produce from your world – where everything is possible – the brush of hope, and to portray in the canvas of life whatever you are capable of dreaming.
- Create your destiny by using your five powers. With the power of thought, visualize in colors everything you wish to materialize in your life. With the power of word, affirm – in the first person and in present tense – all that you wish to make come true in your world. The power of action makes sure that each step you take will lead you to the realization of your dreams. The power of your feelings will give you feedback as to whether you are taking the right path according to your greater good; they are your internal source of guidance. The power of nourishment ensures your physical, mental and spiritual bodies receive the proper nutrition in order to create physical health, wisdom and strength to fulfill your life's plan.
- Remember you can be whatever you desire to be; do what you wish to do; have what you wish to have.
- Free will is the capacity to choose your own creations at any given place and time.

TEST TO CONFIRM YOU HAVE LEARNED THE LESSON:

- ❖ Acquire the habit of finding an easier, better way to do things, whether it is for the things you do at a mediocre level or the things you think you have mastered.

When I left this rune, I had the sensation this place was a sort of conclusion of the previous ones where I had been to; everything sounded like a repetition. However, it was empowering to know I was an unlimited being and that repetition creates reputation. I knew that everything was perfectly related, even when I could not understand the reason why.

I remembered my learning was comprised of forty-eight seals or runes. How long does it take more evolved people to go through their own evaluation? The answer I received was, "a long time," and a song came to my mind which said, "Do not rush, do not rush, there is nowhere to go." As I enjoyed the melody, I entered into the next rune.

FIFTEENTH RUNE
ATTITUDE

- A map is not the territory. Human beings do not live in the territory, meaning, in the reality, but in the map that is made out of that territory.
- Your internal dialogues, or whatever you tell yourself about a certain event, create your attitude.
- You speak to yourself through images, sensations or words.
- Eighty five percent of your success depends on your attitude; then, only with the correct attitude will success be guaranteed.
- It is not the events that make you happy or unhappy; it is your attitude toward them which determines your emotional state of being.
- Before all, after all and above all, attitude is everything.
- Results are results; failure is a judgment about a result; the only way to fail is not to try it again.
- Your attitude conditions your action, your reaction, and therefore your results.
- Recognize everything happens for your own good and that anything is possible; this will assist you in the creation of the right attitude.
- Every human behavior has a positive intention and a context where it is perfectly right.
- Rid your mind of judgments, these arise when you qualify things, and learn to live each moment of your life with the innocence of knowing that it is a new one.

- Expect the best at any given moment of your life and from the people you are with, and so it will be.
- Smile, smile, smile, because life is a fun experience where human beings take their learning way too serious.
- Choose to be above the circumstances; to remain at the same level where the problems originate does not help to find a solution.
- In order to change your attitude, change your altitude.
- A rainy day may be a bad day for many; for others, it is simply nature's way to purify the atmosphere.
- Invoked or not, God is present. Trust, God is in charge. Your mission is to enjoy the way back to Father.
- You can find better attitudes by asking yourself what would a master, or a person that you respect, do in your place. For example, "what would Christ do in my place?"
- The wrong attitude makes you see hell in heaven; darkness in the light; lies in truth; doubt in hope. Later on it only makes you slide further toward the darkness of your own ignorance and it robs you of the opportunity to identify the blessings that you have in life, at any given moment of your life.

TEST TO CONFIRM YOU HAVE LEARNED THE LESSON:

- ❖ Control the internal dialogues; do not try to be right, just go for the result.

- ❖ Tell yourself phrases which will empower you, and learn to see the hidden benefit in every problem.

My deliberations focused on how we tend to complain as an unconscious way to manifest our lack of believe in God. The situation of many like me who feel like we have failed day in, day out, because we live the wrong context of faith, hope, love, understanding and joy, lead me to conclude the big problem continues to be that people believe they can become separate from God. One of those life mottos which in life helped me to have a better attitude was one given to me by a priest, Alberto Hurtado, who, whenever someone asked him how he was doing, his response was: "Happy, sir, happy," and whenever he was having a dilemma, he would ask himself, "What would Christ do in my place?" Based on this attitude, and a great deal of testimonies, he was sanctified by the church.

I remembered this day I felt very ill and someone came calling at my door; my brother answered and said that I was getting better, and when I heard him say that I got angry because I thought it was not the case. What an attitude! How can we prefer to remain anchored to mediocre results just so we can be right, rather than be successful?!

To look at life with the resentment that something can be improved, or we do not like something and we just go around being its worse critic, can sometimes be a painful experience which is why I had to run away from my pain. As a result, I quickly went to the next cloister for the following lesson, and this turned out to be even more perfect and ideal than the previous ones. Slowly, I realized how important it is to have the right attitude in order to control our results, and as I pondered about it, I saw the interesting title of the next rune.

SIXTEENTH RUNE
LEADERSHIP

- You can only lead your own life; a true leader gives up trying to lead others.
- Every human being is equipped with the internal resources which allow him to achieve the desired wellbeing.
- There is a big difference between leading and cheating, or "deceiving." You lead by example and you deceive with words.
- A true leader is willing to conquer himself; his only purpose in life is to fulfill the mission for which he has been created, to live in the light and surrender to the divine will.
- A leader turns into a greater being as he conquers, day after day, his own internal battles, and by his own example other people choose to start the path to their own leadership.
- Apologies and excuses are the biggest obstacles that a human being faces on the road toward their own leadership.
- A leader believes in himself and knows this is the requirement to be it.
- The key words which identify a leader are responsibility, ability to respond promptly, and discipline. These attitudes turn him into a disciple, meaning, one who is willing to learn and constantly applies what he has learned.
- A leader is a visionary who clearly knows the purpose of his existence.

- A leader has no need for followers, for he knows that in order for other people to become leaders they need only to follow their own light.
- The path of the leader can only be walked by one person: the leader. This is why sometimes they appear to be loners.
- The greatest teachers of humanity have been great leaders, loners, and sometimes misunderstood.
- Who cheats or deceives is asking to be followed; he needs a multitude of them in order to assert his predicament. He generally feeds off of the energies of his followers.
- To convince other people is the deceiver's mission, and when he convinces them, he defeats them, diminishing their power and setting a stage where he erects himself as someone superior.
- A cheater, or deceiver, runs away from his loneliness because he cannot bear to be alone with his consciousness, nor is he willing to confront the incoherence between what he preaches and the results he has obtained in life.
- Though a leader does not pretend to guide others, his example inspires many to live their own process of self–knowledge and leadership, to fight their own battles and conquer their obstacles.
- A leader is always guided by divine will and finds that God is the source of his inspiration.
- Every leader must be a visionary who is conscious of his mission, sets goals for excellence, is an enthusiast, filled with energy, knows himself, does a competent job, is perseverant, responsible and generous with his finances, capable of loving unconditionally, humble, a master in the art of communication, displays self–control and internal and external authority because he values his time, his word, and is highly capable of identifying opportunities where others see problems.

TEST TO CONFIRM YOU HAVE LEARNED THE LESSON:

❖ Make a clear mental image of how you would like the world to be thanks to the influence you had in it while you were alive and dedicated your purpose and gifts to the service of humanity. Review this image often.

Many human beings prefer to be manipulated rather than to embark upon the journey of their own leadership; because of this, a true leader is immortalized, makes history – like Mother Theresa of Calcutta or Gandhi – and they have a very close relationship with their Creator, regardless of the religion they profess.

I was able to realize that when people go to music concerts, the kind where they follow an idol, they unconsciously expose themselves to be robbed of their energies; the same thing happens in church. It is a mistake to affirm that to go to a concert or a church may rob you of your energies. This happens when people have turned the artist or the religious leader into an idol, not when people goes to the concert just to enjoy the music, or goes to church because they recognize this is a place which supports their intention to be in contact with their own light; in these cases people become even more empowered.

Each time, a new dilemma arose within me. On this occasion, I was pondering that if a person lives his life according to his purpose, he would undoubtedly turn into a leader. Were there no other options but to either be a leader or be led? It was much more common to follow others rather than one's own light; however, this type of misguided decision puts us on the wrong path, one filled with dependency and vice.

SEVENTEENTH RUNE
COMMUNICATION

- The communicator is responsible for communicating; as such, you must not say that someone did not understand you, rather that you did not make yourself understood.
- When you communicate from the heart, you reach the heart of the people; if you only do it from your mind, you will only reach their mind.
- Every human experience has visual, auditory and kinetic components. Words represent seven percent of communication. Tone, rhythm, volume and pauses constitute another thirty five percent. Physical posture, gestures, movements, body distance and physical contact represent the other fifty–eight percent.
- The way to qualify the quality of a communication is by means of its result.
- Sympathy is the need to gain approval in your communication with other people; Antipathy is the capacity to generate rejection in your communication.
- Empathy is the ability to realize that every time you communicate with someone, you do it with someone who is equal to you.
- The best way to generate empathy is by seeing God in every person, even in yourself.
- The best way to learn to communicate is by learning to listen.
- When you communicate, you are in the first perceptive position; the one who listens is in the second position;

the observer is in the third position. In order to become a master communicator, make sure you shift between the three positions before emitting a judgment and you will realize that everything is originated by you as a communicator.

- You will never have a second chance at making a first good impression.
- When you communicate, love yourself; what this means is that you give the best of you. Love the subject, speak about what you know and listen to what you do not know in order to learn. In addition, love the person who is talking to you, respect his time and do whatever it takes for him to completely understand what you desire to communicate.
- Observe what you tell yourself when you communicate; if inside yourself you consider other people to be smaller than you, expand your view of them and place them at the same level as you are so they can feel more comfortable in your presence and be open to listen to you. If you see them as being bigger than you are, expand your own perceived internal image until you match the other people around; then, you will feel comfortable and inspire credibility. Lastly, if the internal image you have of the person you are communicating with is the same as yours, there will be empathy in your conversation and you will have an excellent communication, because there is no one bigger or smaller than you.
- Make sure your communication is not filled with criticism, condemnation or judgment; and do not complain, for the majority of people are not interested in it while others might find themselves entertained by your mishaps.
- Your mouth should only utter words of blessing, never cursing.

⊚ When you communicate, be sincerely interested in what the other people are saying.

TEST TO CONFIRM YOU HAVE LEARNED THE LESSON:

❖ Understand others before attempting to be understood.

❖ Give yourself the chance to experience a new kind of communication with every conversation.

❖ Listen truthfully, with the innocence of not having the answers beforehand.

"What is it that makes us know what is good for us?" I asked. *"We aspire to accomplish what we want by doing the wrong things. All of this is very easy to understand; however, I almost never put it into practice."*

"The answer is very simple. The chain of knowing–wanting–acting is broken when people act coming from the unconscious recordings and irrational impulses which dominate their lives. To look at and discover the reason why you do something, without judgment and with much love and understanding, will help change the way you act; also, to improve the way you communicate with yourself will help you to improve the way you communicate with others." He said.

I remembered that during my third dimensional life, the more I judged myself the more I judged others, and what I rejected the most about myself was the very same thing I rejected the most about others. The phrase, "Love others as you love yourself," was even more appropriate than before.

To love myself unconditionally in order to be able to love others was my last reflection before making it to the next cloister.

EIGHTEENTH RUNE
DISCIPLINE

- The capacity to constantly learn and apply what is learned.
- To know, want and do. The majority of people know exactly what is good for them and what is not. To *know it* is not enough, they need to have the desire to acquire what they seek and to change what they do not like. It is also not enough to know and to want, you must also do; it is in the doing where most people get in trouble.
- Just as the shortest distance between two points is a straight line, the quickest way between you and your goal is discipline.
- Those who think that it is the application of will power in the doing what transforms the results are mistaken.
- A true disciple requires the presence of a teacher to learn from.
- Recognize everyone is an unconscious teacher to everyone.
- Clearly determine what it is that you wish to learn.
- Once you identify what you wish to learn, choose to learn only from the one who has already obtained such result.

- ❦ A disciple does not follow words but examples; in this way, he makes sure he will not be deceived.
- ❦ The disciple will find the teacher when he is ready to be guided.

TEST TO CONFIRM YOU HAVE LEARNED THE LESSON:

- ❖ Commit only to those things you know you can accomplish, saying 'yes' when you mean it, and saying 'no' when you need to say 'no.'

- ❖ Constantly recreate the habits that you wish to acquire through the repetition of the action and visualization.

- ❖ Associate all you wish to do with pleasure, and you will see how your basic, inner child will support you in the conquest of your dream.

"Is discipline forged through will power?" I asked

"No. That is precisely what this Rune is teaching you." He replied.

"Do you know people who are aware that over eating, smoking, doing drugs and other vices, are bad habits, damaging to their bodies, yet they cannot stop doing it? Have you noticed how time after time they attempt to change the habit without getting the result they want? Could you say these people know what they want?" He asked.

"Yes." I responded.

"Could you say they truly wish to change?" He asked again.

"Yes." I answered.

"Could you judge and say the reason they have not accomplished it is because they lack perseverance?" He asked once more.

"They do not try, and many more will continue to try to change the habit until they are dead." I said.

"With each attempt, instead of strengthening the desire they diminish their self–esteem; they feel they are good for nothing, unworthy of being trusted, have no value, and create a myriad of internal judgments which only lead them to self–punishment."

"Then, what is the problem?" I asked.

"The problem is that their subconscious recordings make them repeat the habit as an automatic, irrational reaction, and they create pre–established, repetitive models of behavior which are stronger than their conscious will to act." He explained.

"What is the solution?" I wondered.

"It is so simple that I will summarize it in three steps:
- *First, the acceptance or recognition that such bad habit has a hold of you.*
- *Second, to love and eliminate all judgments from your mind so you can treat yourself with love and understanding*
- *Third, visualization or creation – through the power of visualization and affirmation – of the successful result which you desire, not of the process."*

"If I follow those three steps I will be able to change my subconscious recordings and transform the habit?" I asked.

"Yes." He replied. *"Constantly visualize the successful outcome of what you desire in colors, like in a movie of which you are the main character; create the perfect atmosphere, lighting, sounds, temperature and predominant feelings, such as happiness and fullness. Decree with a positive affirmation the successful result of what you desire, in present tense and first person. Act and behave as if you already got rid of the bad habit, even more if you are still doing it, for in short time you will see it disappears from your reality." What you have read is the secret to true discipline, and in order to achieve it, you must create the successful result of what you desire. Persevere and maintain yourself in a constant state of creation, meaning, visualize, decree and live as if it already happened. Do not worry about the process or how you will achieve your objective; just hold yourself living the experience of the successful result.*

ƒ

I felt as if I had just connected with deeper levels of wisdom, and because I thought so, so it was. I became so enthusiastic that I quickly went into the next rune in order to further my learning.

NINETEENTH RUNE
HONESTY

- To be honest is to be yourself.
- Many human beings use their knowledge in order to manipulate, and they through life deceiving people and robbing them of their energies. As they acquire more information, they become even more professional at the art of deceiving, and their manipulative games become more subtle, barely perceptible to others.
- An honest person does not fall into such games, for he can clearly identify them.
- Every human being holds an intention or hidden agenda within their actions; to make clearly manifest those intentions is to do away with the veil of illusion, or Maya, and to live in the light.
- At higher density levels, manipulations is done through deceit; at the more subtle levels it can be achieved with a gesture, tone of voice, a flattering comment, a gift, a caress, a hug or a complaint.
- White sorcerers are ascended masters in charge of guiding the spiritual evolution of a planet and inspiring its spiritual leaders.
- Black sorcerers are beings who became stuck in the fourth dimension after death; they generate their power through manipulation of third dimensional people who live in vice, hence making them even more dependent and robbing them of their energy. They feed off of their lack of balance and uncontrolled emotions. They are called 'black' as a way to qualify the fact that they live under their own shadow.

- Many people feel highly inspired by fourth dimensional beings with a low level of evolution, and they do so to such a degree that they cannot even realize they are being manipulated. These deceivers steal the energy of their followers, and in some cases, they even invite religious fanatics to commit suicide or to engage in painful acts of sacrifice in order to support their thirst for glory. As a result, their followers turn into great cheaters or deceivers as well.
- The only way not to be a victim of manipulation is by being honest.
- Cultivate honesty and the shadows will disappear from your life.
- When you read a book, listen to a theme song, go to the theater, observe a painting or enjoy any other kind of artistic expression, check yourself in order to recognize if you feel just as empowered as before, or even more; this is the way to know whether the artist was inspired by the light instead of the darkness.
- You have as many traumas as the number of secrets you hold in life.
- In order to begin walking the spiritual path, it is necessary for the disciple to be completely honest; otherwise he will be lost in the valley of illusion, convinced that he began the spiritual path when in reality he has not.

TEST TO CONFIRM YOU HAVE LEARNED THE LESSON:

- ❖ Freely express, what you think and feel, and give up the need to gain approval.

- ❖ Do not get flattered by people's praise, and do not feel sad when they criticize you.

When I left the cloister it was already night and the atmosphere had changed. I was invaded by a wave of astonishment when I realized that many people, just as me, go through the same experience simultaneously; and it was even more intense to see how many of their faces were familiar to me; however, I did not care about it. I was tired and looking for a place to rest which, even thought I did not know the place, I knew I was about to find soon. I slept so deep that I felt renewed upon awakening, like a newborn to this whole experience.

So, I continued with the process of enlightenment; yes, enlightenment is the best way to define the act of unveiling and understanding so much information.

TWENTIETH RUNE
TIME

- Punctuality is a trait typical of leaders. When you respect other people's time you honor their lives and value their being.
- The present is the moment of power; the past only exists in your memory and the future is being created right now as a result of each one of your choices.
- Make every second of your life count and you will honor your creator.
- You will never get back the time that you have wasted or used unwisely.
- Everything is temporary; as such, this moment will pass. Then, allow yourself to enjoy the experiences you live in the now.
- Measuring time at a quantum level, an hour equals sixty minutes; a minute equals sixty seconds; a second equals twelve instants; and instant equals sixty quarks; a quark equals sixty spins; a spin equals twelve quanta; and a quanta is the minimum amount of energy which can be possibly measured at the same time and space.
- You do not have the years you have already lived, only the ones you have left to live; just as you do not have the money that you earned, but the money left to spend.
- If you chose to live to be eighty years old, you need to take into consideration the fact that you began to consume those years from the moment you were born. No matter what you do, the clock that signals

the passing of your life will not stop until you turn that age.
- Patience is the art of peace, and its science is the biggest vote of confidence and faith that your spirit must develop; remember that everything will happen at the right moment and at the right place.
- Time is relative to who perceives it; a minute of pain is different from a minute of pleasure.
- The more movement there is in your life, the faster that time will pass. If you live a sedentary life, time will be slower.
- Enjoy your present, live intensely here and now so you will honor and bless the privilege of being alive.
- Everything has its time; there is a time for being born and a time to die, a time to sow and a time to harvest, a time to cry and a time to laugh.

TEST TO CONFIRM YOU HAVE LEARNED THE LESSON:

- ❖ Make every second of your life count.

- ❖ Enjoy every moment of your life.

I remembered reading a certain passage in a book: Imagine you are in paradise and you have all that you want, for as long as you want and whenever you choose to have it. Perhaps at the beginning it will be very pleasing, however, with time it will turn into something monotonous enough that you will desire to live there for eternity. Then, you see a button which says 'surprise' and you press it; when you do it, it sends you back to the place where you are today, in the here and now and with your current problems. This invites you to breathe in deeply and be grateful for the present moment: eternity minus one day.

I did not have much to say about this rune. Without notice, I had been robbed of all my time; a second after the least expected day, at the least desired moment. I no longer belonged to that measure of time nor was I conditioned by it.

I recalled an anecdote about Galileo Galilei – a man with a beard and white hair – when someone asked him how old he was, to which he answered that he had between fifteen and twenty. People did not understand what he meant; after a long and silent pause, he finished his answer: "I already spent the others."

TWENTY FIRST RUNE
EXCELLENCY

- Excellency is a road, not a destination.
- Everything can be improved.
- Any one person's achievement can be accomplished by someone else if the task is divided into adequate, small enough segments.
- There are ordinary people who achieve ordinary results, and ordinary people who achieve extraordinary results.
- The one who achieved an extraordinary result was willing to do something extra that the others were not.
- There are no chosen ones; you either choose or disqualify yourself.
- In order to emulate or "model" a result, you need to identify the best one at it, imitate the best, match the best, and be better than the best.
- Learn to identify who is the most appropriate person for you to emulate his strategy or way to obtain results.
- You need to determine the successful result of what you seek and the correct strategy to achieve it.
- The most common mistakes are two: either you identify the wrong person to follow, or you follow the wrong strategy from the right person.
- Focus on what you desire; determine who achieved such result and the precise strategy they used in order to achieve it. This process will allow you to identify

- the tools you need in order to obtain a similar result when you apply the same strategy.
- The resources you need in order to obtain what you want in life are of an internal nature; hence, you were born with them.
- To apply principles of success will undoubtedly lead you to success, or vice versa.
- Mediocre is one that half-believes.

TEST TO CONFIRM YOU HAVE LEARNED THE LESSON:

❖ Read the biography of people who are considered successful or that hold a place of praise in history.

For a long time I held the belief that some people were born for success and others were born to fail. The truth was very simple. I could have achieved the same result that any other person had achieved if I would have only been willing to pay the price; in other words, to learn and apply, systematically, what the other person did and which led them to obtain the desired result.

The name in the following rune gave me a great sense of curiosity, and I imagined this time the lesson would be more of a game.

TWENTY SECOND RUNE
I WIN, YOU WIN

- Nobody needs to lose in order for you to win, nor do you need to lose so that others can win. The game of life is won only when everybody wins.
- If you believe someone needs to lose in order for you to win, then your beliefs are keeping you trapped in the illusion of shortage. Remember, in your world there is enough for every body and in abundance.
- If you believe you need to lose in order for others to win, then your beliefs are keeping you trapped in a game of low self–esteem and lack of worthiness. Remember as the son of God you deserve the best; accept it right now.
- If you believe you cannot win, and you believe others will not be able as well, it is envy that reigns in your heart, with which you are choosing to play the game of "I lose, you lose," and your consciousness is being destructive.
- If you believe everyone must win if you win, or vice versa, then you are dancing in the consciousness of wealth.
- If your thoughts invite you to go beyond the step of "I win, you win," you will enter a world where your relations are for the greater good and with the highest of ends in mind. In this world, the issue of whether you or the other wins is not the main or only purpose; your dealings are ecological in nature; all beings from all kingdoms must win and the result is the best for everyone involved. This will allow you to

live in the spirit, where there is an abundance of light besides richness.

TEST TO CONFIRM YOU HAVE LEARNED THE LESSON:

❖ Abstain yourself from committing to any kind of deal or endeavor, whether it is with yourself or with others, unless every party involved will surely win.

I was premature to judge my passing through this rune; I desired more information, nonetheless, I immediately went to the next cloister. I had displayed this kind of compulsive behavior before, where it seemed as if I was in a rush to get somewhere; however, it was ridiculous to be so frantic because no one was pushing me to go through the cloisters at any given pace.

My life went on this way, rushing my endeavors. I felt cheated by my own self; holding on to the habit of living for tomorrow, I robbed myself of the opportunity to enjoy every moment of my life.

This observation made me slow down the pace, and I began to appreciate the details of everything I was living. The stage for the next lesson appeared in front of me and, before I even went it, I realized that the more one enjoys time and experience, the greater the sensation of eternity to where the limits of space and time actually disappear.

TWENTY THIRD RUNE
THE POWER OF ASSOCIATION

- To select your friendships is to build your future.
- Watch the results obtained by the people you associate with; in the future, yours will be the same.
- Honor yourself when you select your friends; verify and make sure they look and walk toward the same place that you are headed.
- Be selective of what you associate to your senses; select what you read and listen to.
- The best way to determine whether the people you associate with are the right ones is: If you feel better after having shared with them and you also feel more empowered, then it is a convenient association. If the contrary happens though, the only thing you accomplished was losing your energy.
- In five years, you will be the result of what you have read and the people you have associated with.
- You attract into your life people who are very similar to what you are. If you wish to improve your friendships, you need only to improve yourself because equals attract each other.
- Determine the qualities you would like to see in the people you wish to attract into your life, such as honesty, humility, humbleness or optimism; then, work within yourself in order to manifest those qualities and, inevitably, those people will come to you.
- The only mandatory association in life is with your family, in terms of the lessons and teachings they hold

for your own transcendence. To separate from your family is to deny yourself the opportunity to learn your most important lessons.

- Once you complete the lessons that your family will afford you, you will separate from them for a while; not because you are running away from them, but because you have elevated yourself. What this means is you will look at them with much love, and from that new level in which you are, you will accompany and support them in their growth.
- You will be treated by other people in the same way you treat yourself. What you reject the most about yourself will be what they reject the most about you, and what you love the most about you will be what they will love the most in you. Hence, love and accept yourself without conditions so you will associate with people that love and accept you without conditions.

TEST TO CONFIRM YOU HAVE LEARNED THE LESSON:

- ❖ Share your time with the people who are as you wish to be or people that do what you wish to do, or with people who have what you wish to have.

"I think it takes me longer to get out of a cloister and get into the next one, than what it takes me to forget what I have read." I said.

"It is not that way." He replied. *"On the contrary, everything is being recorded in the deepest parts of your being; whenever you need the information, it will simply and naturally manifest in the form of inspiration."*

Will it manifest? When? I did not even know what the use of all of this was. Maybe this is some kind of warning that here is something I will have to repeat and the moment is approaching? I realized, again, that just as I had a thought about something, I could hear the answer coming from within my being, if it was necessary, and each time the process became more natural. It was like talking to myself and at the same time to my inner guide, which possessed all wisdom and gave the best answers to my questions. "It will come when is necessary," I whispered, and then I found myself standing in front of my next level of learning.

TWENTY FOURTH RUNE
THE POWER OF GOALS

- A person who does not know where he is going has already arrived.
- When you set a goal for life, you align all of your energy and creative power toward the achievement of that specific purpose, which will lead you to a quicker materialization of it.
- Once you have a clearly set goal, the law of focus allows you to eliminate any kind of unnecessary information from your mind, which would otherwise deter you from achieving your goal. It also helps to maximize your energy.
- One of the biggest differences between a winner and a loser is his point of reference. A winner speaks about his next goal and focuses on materializing his dreams. In turn, a loser focuses on his past, on what was; he gives up on setting new goals.
- For the loser, anything that happened in the past was the best and his dialogues are constantly wrapped around some remembrance of the past.
- For successful people the best is yet to come, and in order to ensure that it will be so, they lay down the path they need to follow in order to achieve their goals.
- Goals and obstacles are inseparable. Small goals will encounter smaller obstacles; bigger goals will encounter bigger obstacles. If you do not like the obstacles, then do not set any goals; however, if you do not set goals for life, what do you live for? Life is the game of setting goals, and the obstacle allows

you to understand that in the end what was really important was not the achievement of the goal, but the person that you turned into as a result of conquering such goal.
- To live life without setting clear goals is just as boring as starting a game without knowing its rules in order to win. Imagine playing soccer without a soccer goal, to shoot a target without having a target, or playing basketball without a hoop. Does it seem illogical or nonsensical? A life without goals is just like that; it will lack sense and you will be prone to fall into depression.
- Every person who lives a life of vice is lacking goals; every person who lives according to their purpose establishes different goals for different areas of their lives, for they wish to follow a clear road back to Father. Goals are a synonym for a disciple who possesses unquestionable discipline and attitude.
- Just as the shortest distance between two points is a straight line, the shortest distance between you and your goal is discipline.
- Set goals in the spiritual, physical, educational, labor, recreational, economical and human relationships areas of your life.
- Your most sacred goal is to identify clearly the mission for which you were created, and to put yourself to the service of humanity in order to realize your purpose.

TEST TO CONFIRM YOU HAVE LEARNED THE LESSON:

- ❖ Plan ahead of time what you are going to be doing every day, week, month and year of your life.
- ❖ Plan all of your life and your will maximize your time.

What a change of paradigm! In life, I thought that to define goals was for spiritually poor people, materialistic, focused on money and intent on living their life in a box; I thought it was best to be spontaneous, to flow freely and without conditions. I clearly understand now that even to grow spiritually, I needed to set goals; to not do it was a waste of my time.

TWENTY FIFTH RUNE
PROSPERITY

The walls in this cloister were gold plated, inlaid with precious stones; it had a gleaming marbled floor and the roof was detailed with ornate filigree. There were many works of art in some of the walls, and to my surprise, several were quite known on Earth, like Da Vinci's La Gioconda and The Last Super, and Michelangelo's Pietà and The Creation of Adam. The background music was a sublime sound, a perfect match to the classical pieces or art, and we all learned to its rhythm.

I was surprised to see hosts at this beautiful place; it was a first, for I had not encountered them in any of the previous cloisters. These hosts were very amiable and inexplicably humble beings who served tirelessly with a broad smile on their faces; it seemed as if humbleness and service were the two qualities which made one deserving of being there. The humbleness of knowing one is equal to every one else, separated only by the mirage of ignorance, and the sacred gift of service of which we become deserving when we recognize that "the greatest amongst all is the one who serves the most."

Ecstatic, in the midst of so much brilliance and radiance, I found myself in front of the following lesson, which was written in gold plated letters:

- To have money does not mean one has prosperity; on the other hand, to not have money is indeed a sign of lack.

- Prosperity is a consciousness that allows you to bring what you dream about into your life.
- Prosperity is limitless, and it comes from creativity, which is also limitless. Problems with lack are not created by the lack of money; they are the result of lack of creativity. The greatest dreamers of all times fought against skepticism, while the realistic battled with the competition.
- The route to prosperity is: To Be, To Do and To Have.

I found the following title inscribed somewhere inside this wonderful cloister: "Steps to create prosperity." Here, the sensation was superior to what one would experience when entering the most beautiful castle that you could have ever seen. A real palace! I could swear that King Solomon, King Midas or the Magi lived there, along with any other famous person in history who had made a great fortune.

Steps to generate the consciousness of Prosperity:

1. Recognize your inheritance. It is impossible to separate from God; no matter what you do, wherever you are, you are always in God. The more you recognize your union with God, the more you will exhibit His traits: wisdom, power, love and creativity without limits.
2. You were born with a purpose in your heart; your mission is to discover it and put it to the service of humanity. Count your gifts and ask yourself what you would like to do with them, or how you would like to put them to the service of humanity; that is the road to discovering your purpose. Remember there are two roads in life: purpose or vice. It is your choice.
3. Make sure whenever you chose to do something everyone involved in your deal wins. If someone

needs to lose so that you can win, eventually you will also lose, because you and I are one, and just as you are in me, every being in creation is in me. Put yourself in the shoes of the other person and verify that he ends up just as happy as you when you are in your shoes.
4. Always give the best of yourself to life, and demand from life the best for you. It is important to remember that just because you exist, you deserve the best and the blessings have already been given.
5. Enjoy other people's success. If you whole-heartedly enjoy other's success, it is a sign of your knowing and understanding that in the universe there is plenty and in abundance for everyone.
6. Sow constantly what you desire to harvest, because it will inevitably be that way.
7. Learn to give and receive from your heart, without pride, without feeling undeserving, without low self-esteem. To give and receive is an endless circle. When you give, it is God who gives through you to another person; and when you receive, it is God giving you what you deserve through the other person.
8. Tithes. Get used to setting aside ten percent of your income in order to donate it to the place from where you receive your spiritual education. If you are not used to giving a tithe and you desire to control what happens with your money, then at least use this ten percent to give donations to charities. However, if you are used to giving a tithe, send that money to the source of your spiritual lessons, which will turn it into a form of tithe given in advance. Give away an amount of money which you desire for specific issues that you intend to resolve in the future, and you will see how this small act of faith will bring to you, faster

than expected, all the things you wish for. You may also save another ten percent in a bank account that you will never spend, and which will turn into a magnet for money. Even though you may not consciously understand it, this might be one of the greatest secrets for generating prosperity.

TEST TO CONFIRM YOU HAVE LEARNED THE LESSON:

- ❖ Remember your inheritance; recognize you are the son of a King. Your Father is the creator of the universe and you have the right to have the best.

I thought about how much time I lived going against the grain, wanting to have things in order to be able to do or be something; it was hard to live in prosperity. I had not understood that prosperity increases as we work in our Being, in the eternal things like humility, honesty, perseverance, constancy, discipline. Now I understand how people like Jesus Christ, Gandhi, Mother Theresa of Calcutta, and many more, were able to enter into a conscious state of abundance; they did not need to hold on to material things, yet they lacked nothing; it appeared as if everything came to them by mere right of consciousness.

For them, every day brought its own labor; they did not hoard because they knew in their hearts that human beings are like a magnet, and we bring into our lives what by our state of consciousness belongs to us. That right by consciousness is acquired as we advance on our journey, and it is achieved by working on our Being.

As I analyzed the subject, I understood that anybody would be honored to sit at a table with these people, and share their house and food; this is the way to reach a level that transcends matter. Nonetheless, there are those who mistake humbleness for poverty, and they believe that lacking material things is some sort of a great achievement or blessing; in reality, they are very mistaken by assuming sacrifice makes someone worthy of greater blessings. That is to forget the word of Jesus: "What father among you, if his son asks for bread, would give him a stone?" To be humble has nothing to do with being poor; on the contrary, if you are humble and honest, prosperity will come to you by right.

I understood more and more that the levels of prosperity we deserve are related directly to the kind of person that we turn into throughout the journey of life. I thought about all the poverty I saw on Earth, and understood this situation was the result of mistakenly going after richness; I remembered the words of my math teacher, who used to repeatedly say to us that the hardest thing about a problem is to describe it correctly.

It was not easy to leave this place; in the short time I was able to enjoy it I became attached to it. However, other lessons had already taught me that to let go of what we have, and not become attached to it, is a sign of knowing the best is yet to come.

When I left, I was warned that the following runes would be wonderful seeds, and I was advised to let myself flow, to not question and just live the experience as a small child would do, or like an observer without judgment.

TWENTY SIXTH RUNE
THE LAW OF ACCEPTANCE

- The universe works in accordance to thirty–three immutable laws that no one can alter. The first universal, cosmic law is the law of acceptance, in charge of creating harmony in the universe and manifesting love in it.
- This law guarantees your happiness. When you accept yourself as you are, accept your present as a logical outcome of your past beliefs, and as you surrender to enjoying the here and now, you become responsible for your transformation.
- Acceptance is the basis for love; as you accept, you love.
- Accept yourself without conditions. Recognize there is no other one like you in the entire universe, and that difference creates your beauty and makes you special.
- Things are as they are when you like them and when you do not like them.
- Eighty five percent of the problems which worried you never happened. To be worried is to not trust in God. Do not worry, God is in charge. Whether you invoke Him or not, God is always present.
- Preoccupation makes you nervous; being nervous gives you anxiety; anxiety stresses you; stress produces gastritis and gastric ulcers; gastric ulcers lead to stomach cancer, and stomach cancer is an invitation to death. When that moment comes, you

realize everything is impermanent. When you accept, you learn to relax and trust God.
- What you resist persists, and pain is the price you pay for resisting life.
- You will never be given something you cannot handle. At most, you will be tested up to ninety nine percent of your capacity, not a hundred percent.
- Each test is an opportunity to expand your unlimited power.
- Acceptance is the key to transformation. When you accept you solve most of any problem. Acceptance and responsibility give you the ability to transform any result in a timely fashion.
- When you accept people just as they are, you get rid of the resentment in your heart.
- When you accept yourself as you are, you get rid of the guilt in your heart.
- When you accept the circumstances just as they are, you become conscious of how they were created.
- Everything is perfect in the world. You are safe.

TEST TO CONFIRM YOU HAVE LEARNED THE LESSON:

- ❖ Remember nothing is permanent. The moment you have a problem will pass, because everything is transitory.

Acceptance is the key to happiness and harmony. I evoked the many moments in my life in which I abstained from enjoying the results out of my habit to resist life.

I entered into a trance that allowed me to see people who had just arrived to the world of the dead, to the fourth dimension. I perceived the presence of the angel of death, whose function was to invite people to become part of this new world; an invitation many times unconsciously accepted. When I got out of the trance, I decided to take some distance from the process of self-evaluation and proceeded to meditate again; I wanted to recover my energies and I knew this was the best way to do it. I felt a longing. I intuitively knew that just as I missed the detail about the existence of the angel of death, I could have overlooked many other things. The important thing was that I was putting into practice what I had just learned about acceptance, and this drew a slight smile on my face.

TWENTY SEVENTH RUNE
THE LAW OF VIBRATION

- The All is in movement, all atoms are in movement; hence, everything vibrates.
- The various states of matter – solid, liquid and gaseous – vibrate at different rates from dense to subtle; as a result, minerals, vegetables, animals and human beings vibrate.
- Some vibrations are easy to perceive with our human senses; others are less perceptible.
- Energy has a color, sound and vibration.
- With your vibration, you permanently obtain and attract the results you have so far procured in life.
  If you wish to improve your results, you need to improve your vibration; the way to do it is by walking toward the light.
- The highest level of vibration is obtained in the light, while the densest form is obtained in the darkness.
- The people you attract into your life are those who vibrate at a frequency that is similar to yours.
- Every thought, word, action, feeling, emotion or food matter, vibrates at a certain frequency, and it records such frequency in the place where it was created and they are also recorded in your energetic field or aura.
- Your house, office or any other place in general, is imprinted with the thoughts, words, feelings and emotions that originate in such place, and they impregnate the energetic fields of those who find themselves in those places. If you wish to change such

recording, keep a candle lit because fire transmutes everything.
- You are imprinted with the energy of the people and places that you frequent; hence, lean toward sharing and going to places where the light is abundant and is chief in people's consciousness and the atmosphere.
- One of the main functions of fire, water, earth and air, is to change the vibration of all the kingdoms toward the light; use them to your advantage.
- A being of light is recognizable because everywhere he goes, he leaves the place better than how he found it, and he does the same with the people he shares with.
- Let your presence be a constant source of blessing for those who come your way, and whatever comes your way.
- When you go through an unbalancing experience, take a shower and put the clothes you were wearing in the washing machine; this will improve your vibration.
- When you need to go places of low vibration, remember to protect yourself with the blue ray before going in, and use the violet flame on your way out. This will cleanse your energetic fields.
- Let your home be a temple and do not generate negative thoughts in it, for they will be recorded in its walls and it will reprogram you on a daily basis with this energy. Focus only on keeping thoughts of the light; in this way, your life will be always filled with much love and happiness at the end of your workday, and it will be your place of rest and peace.
- Walk barefoot in nature every once in a while, and she will absorb any negative energy flowing from you.

TEST TO CONFIRM YOU HAVE LEARNED THE LESSON:

- ❖ Breathe in the open air.
- ❖ Walk in nature.
- ❖ Make bonfires.
- ❖ Bathe in the oceans and rivers.

Many times throughout my life I told myself that I would go somewhere to spend the day, however, a few minutes after having arrived I would be overtaken by impatience and leave. Other times it was the opposite; when I said I would only be staying for five minutes, I stayed for way longer than that. I understand now it had to do with the specific vibration of each particular place.

I contemplated something new: why do I not feel hungry in this place? My physical body did not demand anything; it was enough to meditate or switch to a new activity in order for my body to recover its energy.

TWENTY EIGHTH RUNE
THE LAW OF CYCLES

- Everything ebbs and flows. Everything has its periods of advancement and recession, ascent and descent; everything moves like a pendulum, in which the amount of movement that occurs from the center toward the right, is the same amount of movement that occurs from the center toward the left.
- Everything comes back to us; what you give out of love and without an agenda comes back to you increased and quicker than you can imagine.
- In order to your power, life will give you the opportunity to experiment everything through the cycles.
- Everything will come back to you as a means to invite you to confirm the lessons learned.
- The future of human beings is very easy to predict, because the experiences repeat themselves.
- Coming back will allow you to live the law of compensation.
- Your experiences will repeat themselves periodically. You will be able to determine accurately the length of these periods once you have reviewed the history of your past.
- Everything manifests in a movement of coming and going, and as such, you will have moments of sadness and others of happiness.
- To determine your cycles is to prepare for your next changes.
- Your emotional state of being will constantly change; you will go from being optimistic, to being pessimistic;

you will go through the positive, neutral and negative states of being.
- The day renews itself every twenty–four hours; your emotional states renew themselves cyclically every twenty–eight days; and the Earth, every three hundred and sixty five days.
- In order to be clear about the mechanics of your life cycles, it is important to keep a daily record.

TEST TO CONFIRM YOU HAVE LEARNED THE LESSON:

- ❖ Make a detailed observation of the days when you feel optimistic and the days when you feel sad; write down how you felt during the day in a sheet of paper and you will notice your emotions will repeat themselves every certain periods of time; as a result, you will become clear on how to begin your next day.

- ❖ Keep a daily record of the predominant feelings which you experience throughout the day; at the end of the month, make a graph in order to observe the behavior of your recorded emotional states of being.

"Could it be that cycles are the key factor by which fortune tellers were able to determine what would happen to us in the future? Everything has a cycle; the moon, the movement of the stars, the seasons, the hours of the day, the days of the week, and the months of the year. How is that possible?! Everything is so simple, yet we are so closed to its understanding!

"It is good that you are realizing certain details." I heard my inner voice say. *"Each rune provides information according to the stage of evolution of each being and his capacity to comprehend it."*

"Are they the same forty eight runes for everybody?" I asked.

"No. Although everyone goes through forty eight runes, the process is more complex for some than for others, because the more you advance in your own self-knowledge, the more consciously aware you become about any given subject, or the more prepared you are for receiving an advanced level of knowledge. Did it ever happen to you that every time you went back to read the same book, the more sense you could make of it over the course of time?"

"Yes." I answered. *"But I would like to know everything now."*

"It would be of no use." My inner voice said. *"Because you obtain information, but it is the experience of it what will lead you to your own wisdom, the state in which light comes into your life and there is a surge of understanding."*

"And what will happen?" I questioned.

"What will happen is that you will finish this cycle of lives and deaths; you will rise above the law of cause and effect; everything you sow will be positive and when that time comes you will be an ascended master."

"Does that mean all human beings will eventually, at some point in our evolution, turn into beings of light, teachers of wisdom like the saints or great masters of humanity?" I asked.

"In reality, all human beings are beings of light; some have chosen to share their shadow and others their sanctity."

"Will I eventually turn into someone who will share only his light, in the way of the great masters like Jesus, Buddha or Mohammed?" I wondered.

"Yes, everything in life is evolving; first you learn, then you teach."

"I do not understand much."

"Do not rush." My inner voice said. "The following lessons will help to clarify further and find the answers to many of your questions."

TWENTY NINTH RUNE
THE LAW OF FOCUS

- The direction in which you look is the direction in which you are headed.
- You are where your attention is.
- Focus your thoughts only on what you desire to bring into your life.
- Focus your words only on what you wish to materialize in your life.
- Only you have the power to decree one word only, and at the same time keep one single thought in your mind, so make sure that such word and such thought are coherent with what you wish to materialize in your life.
- Keep your attention focused on prosperity and it will reign in your life.
- Keep your attention focused on happiness and you will be a happy being.
- Keep your attention focused on health and you will be a healthy being.
- Keep your attention focused on truth and you will be an honest being.
- Keep your attention focused on your blessings and on blessing others, and you will turn into a light beam.
- Keep your attention focused on peace and harmony will reign in your life.
- Keep your attention focused on success and you will be a successful being.
- Keep your attention focused on excellence and you will evolve much faster.

- Keep your attention focused on your continuous improvement, in the knowledge of the self and the eternal, and you will notice how all limitations will disappear from your life.
- Keep your attention focused on the light and the greater good will reign in your life.
- Autosuggestion is the art of spending more time focusing your attention on what you desire to see in your own sphere of reality, and as a result of it, it will materialize much faster.

TEST TO CONFIRM YOU HAVE LEARNED THE LESSON:

❖ Dedicate some time to keep your attention focused on a specific subject in order to develop your concentration abilities.

It sounded so easy, that just by focusing on what we wanted everything we disliked about our world would simply disappear from our reality. To think of all the people who watch soap operas in which evil and deceit are the main subject, and they keep their attention focused on that. I wonder when the day will come when we will be taught the importance of focusing only on what we wish to materialize? And where does this human need to feed on the negative come from? However, the fact that I was receiving this information implied there has to be a world in existence where people do not watch or hear soap operas, or unsettling news; maybe a more evolved planet.

The day sparkled with such a special and perfect energy that the landscape, filled with multicolored roses garden –which I had seen many times before – made me reconcile with myself and accept.

I walked as calmly as I could and stopped in front of the sign of the next rune, and I wondered whether I should go in or not, or maybe I should just stay outside for a little longer and enjoy the lovely morning. In the end, what was the rush? After a while, I continued my journey; I had only taken a few steps in when I realized I had not read the name of the rune; I went back quickly and saw the name written in the sign:

THIRTIETH RUNE
THE LAW OF POLARITY

- The All has polarities of the same essence, which are part of the same learning.
- The law of polarity says that once you experience one side of a polarity, you have the obligation to experience the other side or pole of it, so you may live the experience in its totality.
- As such, you will experience happiness as well as sadness, loneliness as well as companionship, resentment as well as forgiveness, war as well as peace.
- What appears to be bad can turn into the greatest of your blessings.
- You live in a relative world. Nonetheless, your mind invites you think in dual terms until you realize that nothing is good or bad, just relative to the angle from which you observe it.
- Light and shadow, day and night, man and woman, heat and cold, positive and negative, love and hate, are all polarities of the same All.
- You hate a person so much and you may end up loving her. The darkest part of the night is right before dawn; nothing is permanent; everything is transitory, from the shadow to the light.
- You may change the polarities by your mere presence; for example, if you go to a place where there is disease, and you know that in nature there are both sickness and health, put your attention on

the polarity of health and the sickness in the environment will disappear.

- If you feel happy when you are being praised, or feel sad when you are criticized, it means you are playing the puppet; someone that is dragged from one polarity to another by other people's whim. Live in your own neutrality, turn into the observer. Do not let yourself be flattered by people's praise, nor diminished by their critics, and peace will reign in your life.
- Give all of yourself when you participate in life; live as if every day is the last of your existence. It is better to sleep tired than frustrated. Detach from the end result, and when duality takes over you and invites you to judge, place yourself beyond the polarity, in a neutral place where everything is perfect.
- The critical mass or predominant vibrations tend to trap you; change polarity when you find yourself stuck in a vibration which brings results that are different from what you want.

TEST TO CONFIRM YOU HAVE LEARNED THE LESSON:

- ❖ Become your own, neutral observer.
- ❖ Contemplate both the action and the doer without judgment.

Maybe everything can be summarized as *not desiring*. What would be the purpose of life without desires? I wondered, and I understood that maybe the key lies in not becoming attached to our desires. Polarity opened the door to many questions in my mind: If we have to go through all of the different types of polarities, will we live swinging between one and the other until we achieve mastership? The rune said it very clearly: the ideal state is one of neutrality, to be the observer without judgment and to live in the light of God.

There again I was questioning, and coupled with the feeling of not being able to make sense of this experience I was prompted to ask my internal being what it all meant.

"It is an advanced lesson in spirituality designed for those who, like kids, are able to look at life without judgment. One day, all of these will be so familiar to you like any other kind of information you posses at the present moment."

"What is the use of all these information?" I asked.

"So you may know that your journey goes from darkness toward the light; in order to get you closer to your unlimited power."

"And how do I do it?" I wondered

"You have been doing it for millions of years."

✍

What is done is done. Millions of years seemed like a long time in order for me to decide not to enjoy the journey at this stage. Hence, I began humming songs and recalled memories that filled me with great joy.

THIRTY FIRST RUNE
THE LAW OF KARMA AND DHARMA
OR
CAUSE AND EFFECT

- Every human being molds his destiny according to what he thinks, feels, speaks, does, feeds and says to himself.
- You are responsible for your destiny, and as such, for the results you get.
- There is no such thing as a coincidence; there is only causality.
- You have created everything that happens, by means of what you have planted.
- Karma means Cause; dharma means effect. Everything has an effect, and all effect is the result of a previous cause.
- You are constantly creating your future, in your eternal present, here and now, consciously or unconsciously.
- If you wish to control your future, you must control your present creations.
- If you wish to be a prosper person you must think, talk, feel, act, and feed your body, mind and spirit like a prosperous being does; the same applies to anything else you wish to create in your life.
- Nothing happens randomly; every event that you evoke, whether consciously or unconsciously, makes sense in its own way.

- To consider one is the victim of the circumstances is only the fruit of ignorance.
- Your poverty or wealth, your health or sickness, your happiness or sadness, they are all your creations and you can always change them.
- Karma is what you sow and dharma is what you harvest; as a result, dharma is the fair harvest which is picked on the day your crop is ripe.
- Some of your results belong to previous lives' creations, because you have all of eternity in order to harvest what you sowed.
- Earth is a school where wingless angels learn lessons in order to recover their wings and go back home.
- In life, you will get what you create, allow or provoke.
- You move all the way from unconscious ignorance to unconscious wisdom, going through conscious ignorance and conscious wisdom; all of these through your causes and effects.
- To regret does not mean that a lesson has not being learned, only that you are close to completing the learning and a part of your memory becomes more sensitive, meaning, it prepares you for your next harvest.
- There is such thing as justice in life; to believe the opposite is ignorance of this natural law.
- The law of God never fails.
- Life does not punish, it teaches. When you are going through an unpleasant experience, ask yourself what it is you need to learn from that experience, for once you have learned the lesson your experiences will change.
- Nobody knows something without first having failed at several attempts; as such, no body learns to love without first having hated; to be honest without first being dishonest; to fly without first having stumbled.

- Life is a continuous learning process and walking from the darkness towards the light.
- Be thankful for everything that happens to you because from this perspective your only option is to learn. Also, be careful when making decision in the present because they create your future.
- The moment of power is the present.

TEST TO CONFIRM YOU HAVE LEARNED THE LESSON:

❖ Be conscious of what you sow and work to improve it according to what you expect from life.

This rune contained so much information that it would take a long time in order to understand it all. That said, I realized I had spent a lot of time, or better, many lives trying to learn about it.

Although in the third dimension I stubbornly thought there was such a thing as injustice, now I understand that life is fair. I understand is fair for a child to be born blind, with brain problems, AIDS or any other kind of physical limitation; that a child would be born in one home rather than another; that a child would have known his parents or not; because whether he likes it or no, he had already planted those seeds and this life was only affording the harvest.

Besides, it was important to admit we are all innocent; we act in the best way we can, as best we know, and if something happens to someone it is because it is appropriate, meaning, he is only reaping what he sowed. Even though it seemed difficult, I had to understand that life is in constant evolution and every person is at some stage on their own journey – I was at some point in my own road – and in the end, we would realize we all have to walk that road and learn the available lessons, though everyone chooses a different variation of it in order to learn the same lesson.

I could not accept that if I was robbed, it was because I had robbed someone else; and that if I was not robbed it was because I had already learned the lesson; and the difference between a thief or a murdered and myself was that I had done it first, and through my own sowings and harvests I had had enough of the results, I had become aware of the circumstances and began to walk the road of my own evolution choosing to sow honesty and life.

"What have you learned?" My inner voice asked me.

"That I know nothing." I automatically answered.

"Which means you are on the right track."

"Which means I have a lot of questions to ask." I felt I was being aggressive and intolerant in my communication. However, I did not judge myself for this, I just accepted it.

"Well, now is the time to address those questions." Said my inner voice.

"First, I think it is completely unfair that we should pay for something we did in another life and which we do not even remember."

"Life does not punish, it teaches you," I heard my inner voice say, *"and it teaches when the apprentice is ready to learn. Just because you forget that you owe a debt does not mean you do not continue to owe it; in other words, if at the moment you incur the debt you are dressed in a certain way, would it be fair for you to tell the collector you do not owe him a debt anymore just because the moment you bumped into him you are wearing something else? Remember,*

you are today the summary of all of your evolution; you act in the best way you know and you also react in the worst way you know."

"I also think it is unfair for kids to pay for the sins of their parents!"

"I think the same; even more, no one ever pays something he does not personally owe, and if the learning is for the father, it does not make sense that the son should suffer the consequences. What happens is that parents and kids attract each other because they have similar lessons to learn."

"What about events which affect a lot of people?" I asked.

"In such cases, there is a collective lesson to learn."

"I met a lot of people whose lives were very pleasant and who reaped very good harvests even though what they sowed was not exactly adequate. What happens in those cases?" I wondered.

"Throughout life, people go through periods of repent in which they make it a point to perform good deeds, and because the lessons have not been learned yet, they continue to fall again and again. They sow insanity and unbalance even though in the past they might have planted sanity and equilibrium; and so, there comes the time when they reap from the sanity, and other times they reap from the insanity, independently from what they might be sowing at the moment. Do not worry about it or envy them."

"Does this mean that it works like the law of an eye for an eye?" I questioned my inner voice.

"No," It said, *"This is something other than revenge; it means that the experiences will continue to happen to you until you learn the lesson. Hence, the question that you should be asking yourself with every situation is: what do I need to learn from this experience? And throw away mistaken affirmations and claims such as: why is this happening to me?"*

I pondered and then asked, *"If someone robs or harms me in any way, is that person doing me a favor, and as such, he turns into a master who helps me to resolve some of my karma?"*

"It is true that if it happens to you it is because it is appropriate for you. However, nobody is a conscious master to anybody and we are all unconscious masters to everyone. What this means is that, if someone hurts you, even though he is teaching you by giving you the opportunity to feel with your own flesh and blood what you had already done, that person is also sowing – in an unbalanced way – what he will surely reap in the future. The person is not conscious of the lesson he is giving to you. On the contrary, conscious masters or more evolved beings, teach only through love.

ƒ

I wanted to go back to a previous rune, but I was not allowed to do so. The explanation was that one of the rules of the game is I can only enter each cloister once, and every one learns the lessons according to where they are. I left a bit angry, I must say, and I saw that across from where I was there was another hall to where I was supposed to go.

THIRTY SECOND RUNE
THE LAW OF REVERSIBILITY

- Life's experiences repeat themselves over and over until the lessons are learned; the way to know this is by being aware of the way you react to them.
- Reversibility means to repeat a process or experience because the moment we experienced it in the past, we did not learn the lesson.
- Reversibility guarantees you will not move to a higher lesson until you have learned the previous one.
- If your life becomes monotonous it means that you are someone who learns at a very slow pace; whether you want it or not, you will learn.
- The difference between two human beings lies on how fast they can learn and the number of lessons learned.
- You attract into your life people who exhibit similar behaviors to yours, so that you may learn from what you accept and reject about them.
- What you accept or reject about someone else, if you watch carefully, is the same thing you either accept or reject about yourself.
- Remember you do not see the world as it is, but how you are.
- When the lessons have been learned, the world around you changes; sometimes you change your physical location or friends; other times your friends change the way they relate to you.
- Always welcome change, and remember everything that will happen to you will be for your greater good.

- There are lessons to be learned in every aspect of your life, whether it is in matters of the spirit, the physical, work, study or finances, relationships and entertainment.
- Continuous learning yields continuous improvement.
- Your personal transformation is proof that you are learning.
- What you excel at is the fruit of many failed attempts which have created in you the experience of it.
- Excellence is a road, not a destination. For the duration of your vital cycle, you advance on that road as you learn every lesson available to you.

TEST TO CONFIRM YOU HAVE LEARNED THE LESSON:

> ❖ Become conscious of the events that repeat themselves in your life and how you have created them.

I knew about the law of reversibility; there was a time when someone explained it to me so well that it was a wonderful way for me to make sense of many things. It is like going to the theater to watch the same play several times, but each time played by different actors; we realize that in every single case we are looking at the same argument. The same thing happens with each aspect of our lives. I remember on one occasion I broke up with a girlfriend from whom I rejected many things, and shortly after I met another woman who, at the moment, I believed could be my ideal companion; after spending some more time getting to know her, I realized she was playing the same roles as the previous one. I had only changed the illusion called form. Work is another environment where the law of reversibility was evident. Very frequently, people change jobs because they cannot stand their co-workers or their boss, but they fail to wonder why they find themselves involved, yet again, with people who display the same kind of behaviors they rejected from their previous co-workers.

On the other hand, the purpose of life is not to run away, but to transcend. When a person transcends an experience, the universe makes sure that the appropriate changes take place. Nevertheless, coming back to the subject of work, when a person leaves his job because he has found a better option, his co-workers will miss him and he leaves an empty hole. These are typical cases of transcendence. The same happens with friendships and romantic relationships.

For example, in some cases and without realizing it, some people with whom we have been very close at one point in our life seem to simply disappear from our environment, and we even forget their faces and their names. What this means is that in this particular part of the movie of our life, such actors are either not important or they do not have a part to play.

Yes, life is a movie and each person is the main character – from their own perspective, each one creates their own argument, drama or passion, success or failure, joy or tragedy, prosperity or lack – where the important thing is to admit that to change from within is the only way to change our environment.

I tried to imagine what could be happening in the world of the living, what day of the year it was, what would my friends be creating or how many of them were stuck repeating the same lessons and complaining about how boring life is. Just like when you repeat a subject in school and you complain about how boring it is to study the same thing again and again. How tedious having to repeat the same lessons!

Feelings of contemplation and longing kept me company; in my mind, I could hear the following words resonating: "you either learn or you repeat it," and on that beautiful day I only managed to laugh once more, a laughter which seemed to have shaken the skies, or so I thought. I tried to ignore what I was feeling and what was flowing from my mind; I was determined to enjoy this magical moment. I made an effort to concentrate on the present moment and it was an unforgettable experience. I discovered the sky, nirvana, paradise. Nothing worried me. I simply enjoyed. I felt everything and I saw every landscape as a unique experience, absolutely without comparison.

THIRTY THIRD RUNE
THE LAW OF SYNCHRONICITY

- Synchronicity is the art of being in tune with what is being lived, and the understanding of the *why* and *what for* of life.
- The synchronicity of life allows you to understand that everything is perfect; each event you attract into your life, as well as each person who comes your way, has a specific message, a lesson, and a specific purpose in your life's plan.
- To become sensitive is to understand each message.
- Your lessons are always the right ones, and they happen at the right place and with the right people.
- Life does not proceed with mistakes or at random, because everything is perfect.
- To understand the synchronicities is to awaken from ignorance in order to live with self–assurance.
- The perfection of life invites you to accept that every encounter, no matter how casual or irrelevant it may seem, carries a message for you.
- Your family, your friends, your work, the place where you live, what you choose to learn or teach, is all part of your very own synchronicity.
- Personal synchronicity is conditioned by group synchronicity.
- To look around you and to deny or reject what you are experiencing is an unconscious process by means of which you rob yourself of the opportunity to gain a lesson in life, and all because of your ignorance of how the law or synchronicity works.

- Everything is connected in the universe beyond the boundaries of your senses; each thought, word or action of yours is seeking to materialize itself at the right moment and in the perfect circumstance. This is the law of synchronicity in action.
- Life does not proceed by will, but by means of creation. Create from your thoughts, words and actions and trust the law of synchronicity will attract your most beautiful dreams. You need only to wake up in order to access the language of the universe and watch out for the signs.
- The universe is interrelated by means of waves and particles, energy and matter. Everything is united; there is no void or separation, neither in space nor in time, which is only the illusion perceived by your senses.
- You are a part of a whole and your decisions affect the universe in general, as well as the process of collective creation, even though in some cases you may think that to be insignificant.

TEST TO CONFIRM YOU HAVE LEARNED THE LESSON:

❖ Be conscious of everything you attract into your life.

I immediately recognized that what people call synchronicity is in fact Perfection, precisely because they refuse to admit to perfection. One needs only look around in order to see that everything obeys such synchronicity. It is enough to analyze any aspect of life in order to discover that it only belongs to one of those perfect coincidences; for example, to be in one place at a certain time and to run into a person who inspires us to get to know her and share with her, and with time come to the understanding that such person ultimately changed our life. The same happens when you start working a new job, or begin a new area of study.

I noticed how, even though I was not aware at the moment, finding a person always made sense in my life, because through that person I would later connect with other people or I would arrive to a new place, or I would change my opinion with regards to making a decision in a way which would end up being in my favor. For example, one day back in my home city – with a population of over nine million people – as I made my way up the main street in order to get a cab, the cab driver completely ignored my signals to stop and he just kept going. Once I was done complaining about it, I noticed standing right beside me was this cousin of mine whom I had not seen for over fifteen years, and he immediately recognized me. From that moment on, we began spending time together, and in the end, the encounter turned into a very important event for him because it helped him to improve his quality of life. Another time, on a trip from Santiago de Chile to Miami, I made an eight days stop in Venezuela in order to visit with some family; on the fourth day, and on a Wednesday morning, my younger brother asked me to accompany him to the store and right there I met the woman who later on would become my wife. On another occasion, as I attended a conference about the growing issues in the jail system, I had the idea of doing the same. Sometime after, teaching seminars came to be the job which fulfilled my spirit the most.

In order to perceive the synchronicity one needs only to be willing to accept how each experience or person we attract into our lives brings a powerful message into our lives, and that in order to discover it or understand it we need to learn the most important language: the language of life.

Now I wondered if I would actually be able to enter into all of the forty–eight runes, or if some of them were reserved for higher levels of existence. This time I received no answer, but I did not worry about it either; I simply kept going.

THIRTY FOURTH RUNE
LIGHT AND SHADOW

- Light and shadow. It is impossible to leave yourself out, you either act coming from your light or from your shadow.
- Choose to invoke the light for the greater good and the highest purpose at any given moment of your life, and the state of confusion will disappear from your existence.
- When you invoke the light, whatever is contrary to love will come to the surface in order to be healed.
- There are beings of light and shadow beings.
- The light illuminates your road. It enhances the joy you get out of your learning and generates a sense of understanding that comes from within you. As such, problems turn in situations which stimulate your spiritual development.
- The shadow obscures your understanding; it causes you to believe you are the victim of the circumstances; it limits you, prevents you from moving forward and leads you to depression and dependency.
- The purpose of the beings of light is to guide you from your shadow towards your light; they invite you to get to know yourself, to discover love, the power and the light that you carry within.
- Beings who inhabit the shadow feed off of your energy, they rob you of it, and in order to do this they keep you hooked on any kind of vice; they create false emotions and make you become dependent.

- Beings of light have a hierarchy system. *Archangels*, creators of the angels and carriers of absolute knowledge of good and evil; *The Elohim*, creators of form and guide to the elementals, who posses a seventy five percent knowledge of the light and one hundred percent knowledge of the shadows; *Ascended Masters*, in charge of guiding the spiritual evolution of planets and who already got out of the cycle of life and death, they posses twenty five percent knowledge of the light and one hundred percent knowledge of the shadows; and *Humans*, who posses five percent knowledge of the light and one hundred percent knowledge of the shadow.

TEST TO CONFIRM YOU HAVE LEARNED THE LESSON:

- ❖ Invoke the light to help you through every major decision in your life, as well as every day when you wake up in the morning.

Light, shadow, hierarchies? These were all new to me. Hence, this time I will need to get some answers to my questions, and my sacred part was right there in order to warn me about something in particular concerning this rune.

"When you begin a new subject of study, the process consists of receiving new information, and then you reject it, analyze it and question it until you either turn it into light or shadow."

"I do not understand." I said to my sacred voice.

"We turn it into light when we understand the information, we put it to the test and we apply it, and then, as a result of it, we accomplish the results we want."

"Does that mean we do not usually apply all of the information, at all times?" I asked.

"Information which does not help you to improve yours or other people's quality of life is only there to strengthen the dominion of the intellect over your life, which, even though it may hold the correct answer to something, does not inspire you into action; on the contrary, it makes you arrogant by means of the ego which is being fed by your illusions; it takes you from the light and brings you into the shadow."

"I know people who accept information without hesitation, without corroborations." I said.

"And from their ranks there comes the fanatics, the ones that fan the flames of discord and go through life manipulating others in order to attract followers; this allows them to feel more secure about what is only a theory in their own lives.

"Can one go from being a fanatic, to having wisdom?"

"Yes, and you will cease to be a fanatic; you will stop wanting for others to follow you; you will not need to convince or scheme because now the light is in you and the shadow will have disappeared."

"What should I be aware of?" I asked intrigued.

"You are about to enter the cloisters which will clarify much of this apparently new information, therefore I invite you to be aware of the details and do not disregard anything; just say: 'For now, I do not understand. The moment will come when the light will illuminate me.' The light is to recognize the truth."

"What is that truth?" I wondered.

"That there is no such thing as shadow, only the absence of light. When you become firm in your life about the truth, or you invoke the light, you will dance to the rhythm of the natural laws and you will live according to your purpose."

I still wanted to understand something. *"Speaking about hierarchies, what is the role of the Holy Spirit in all of it?"*

"It is the highest level of light. When you invoke the Holy Spirit you are asking for your vibration to reach the highest of levels, so your results may change and your wishes will come into alignment with the Divine Will."

"And what does that mean?" I replied.

"It means that you must wish and do everything from your Holy Spirit."

"My Holy Spirit? You mean I have one?" I was surprised.

"Just as you inhabit God and is impossible to separate from Him, you may invoke the holy aspect of the whole that is in alignment with the greater spirit, the great spirit of creation, and inhabit in Him."

"What about Jesus, the Christ?"

"He is an ascended master who came to teach about the power of love and to activate the Christ energy in human beings."

"Could you give me a better explanation?" I asked.

"All beings have a Christ energy which resides within their hearts; when they visualize it, they activate the energy that creates the path toward truth and life; through it, Creator and the created are one."

I was interested, so I kept asking; *"He came to teach us that we all have this Christ energy? Meaning, people did not know about it?"*

"Just a few of them knew. Even in these times a lot of people believe that the Christ energy is outside of them, even though in theory they follow the path of looking for Christ within their hearts."

"How can a person properly activate such energy?" I wondered with curiosity.

"First, he must ask to be forgiven for all of his wrong doings, whether they were done in thought, word, act or by omission throughout his eternity, whether he remembers it or not. Then, he must send his forgiveness to everyone who caused him any harm. This forgiveness must come from the heart, with no charge, just love and understanding."

"And then, what?"

"Every time he does that, he will feel closer to the presence of God and his dreams will materialize much faster. Very soon, you will learn something much more novel to you about the light; you will learn how the light influences you on a constant basis, and each day certain aspects of the light influence your energy. One day you will be able to see the quantity and the quality of the energy that is put out by all beings in all kingdoms, and it will become a unique and universal language where honesty will reign."

I felt my brain was fuming hot and congested, and my heart was pounding faster than usual. I wanted to rest, but my curiosity was stronger than all of it. I decided to continue, and I felt just as excited as a little kid who is about to discover something new.

THIRTY FIFTH RUNE
FIRST DAY

- Sunday. Mayor influence from the Sun, the astral king.
- Color Blue. All the different shades of blue are predominant on this day.
- Archangel Michael, being with the greatest knowledge about the light and the shadow, whose sword of freedom separates the good from the bad.
- Elohim Hercules, known in mythology as the God of Strength, creator of all the elementals on this day.
- Ascended Master El Morya, one of the masters in charge of the spiritual evolution on planet Earth. Before he ascended, some of his most renowned incarnations were as King Arthur, Saint Thomas More and Thomas Moore, an English poet from the XIX century.
- *DO* is the solfeggio syllable that holds the frequency of this day.
- These beings of light inhabit the temple of Darjeeling in India.
- Faith, hope, happiness, will, protection, perseverance, strength, courage, discipline and persistence, are qualities that a person obtains when he works the predominant energies of this day with the light; working with the shadow, he will only get unrest, fear, insecurity, weakness, pride, submission, lack of discipline and sadness.

TEST TO CONFIRM YOU HAVE LEARNED THE LESSON:

- ❖ Feel the positive aspects of this ray at the same time that you become aware of your breathing at any given time of the day.

Before I left this cloister, I asked my higher self to explain the information further, because the subject was something rather new to me.

"The day of strength and faith is Sunday. If you learn to breathe and visualize this ray all around you, your inspiration and wisdom will vibrate in different levels of knowledge."

"Sunday is for resting, sleeping in and watching the T.V." I replied.

"It is a mistake to think that you rest because you stop doing; you rest when you change activities. Those who think they are resting when they are not doing anything tend to wake up even more tired."

"Then what is the right thing to do?"

"There is no right or wrong. Is just that if you spend Sunday going out sunbathing, doing sports and taking advantage of the time in order to nurture your spirit, then your week will be filled with more energy than what can be produced by spending the whole day watching the T.V."

"But one can do sports, go sunbathing and nurture one's spirit on any other day of the week." I questioned.

"Yes, but what I meant to say is that Sunday is the best day to charge yourself with energy."

I went out with the intention of moving on to the next cloisters as fast as I could, with no pause in between, as I wanted to learn about the other days of the weeks without any kind of interruption; right at the entrance of the next cloister I was perplexed to find a golden angel which looked like the sun. I looked back at the rune I was leaving behind and, ooh! Surprise! There was a sky blue angel. I was so amazed that I wondered how many more details I had missed and how many more lessons I had left incomplete because I was not paying attention. But this was not the time for regrets. I needed to continue.

THIRTY SIXTH RUNE
SECOND DAY

- Monday. Mayor influence from the Moon.
- The color Yellow and all of its shades are predominant on this day.
- Archangel Jophiel.
- Elohim Casiopeia, known in mythology as the God of wisdom, he creates all the elementals on this day.
- Ascended master Lanto, one of the masters in charge of the spiritual evolution of planet Earth.
- *RE* is the solfeggio syllable with the frequency of the energy during this day.
- The beings of light who govern this ray inhabit in the temple of the Rocky Mountains, which are shared by the United States of America and Canada.
- Understanding, knowledge, wisdom, intelligence and enlightenment are typical traits of the light, and these are obtained by means of working with the predominant energy of this particular day; working in the shadow you will only get intellectual pride, vanity and ignorance.

TEST TO CONFIRM YOU HAVE LEARNED THE LESSON:

- ❖ Feel the positive quality of this ray, at the same time that you become aware of your breathing at any given moment throughout the day.

"Let us do this in sections." I uttered to my inner being. *"Does this mean that each day is influenced only by a specific type of energy?"*

"No." I heard my sacred being say. *"All of the energy and its influence are present every single day. However, for each day there is a greater influence of a certain type of energy. Every time you have a thought of doubt, insecurity or weakness, it is recorded with a dark blue color in your aura or energetic field, hence attracting these type of emotions into the reality of your world. When you have faith, strength and will power, it is reflected in your energetic field as a sky blue color which attracts those kinds of feelings into your life. You are learning the meaning of every color."*

"Good." I said. *"Can I feel scared on a Tuesday, for example?"*

"Of course, and this too will be recorded in your aura with a dark blue color. What happens is that as you consciously learn this information, you may fill yourself with the polarity of higher vibration contained within the energy of the particular ray for the day in which it is predominant."

ʄ

In front of me there was another rune; at the entrance, a rose-colored angel. He was looking at me, and his face and smile were sweet and filled with hospitality.

THIRTY SEVENTH RUNE
THIRD DAY

- Tuesday. Major influence from the planet Mars.
- The predominant color on this day is Rose in all of its different shades.
- Archangel Chamuel.
- Elohim Orion, known in mythology as the God of Love and Attraction, creator of all the elementals of love.
- Ascended Master Rowena, one of the masters in charge of the spiritual evolution of planet Earth.
- *MI* is the solfeggio syllable that holds the frequency of this day.
- The light beings who teach these lessons inhabit the temple at Chateu de Liberté in Marseille, France.
- Love, freedom, detachment and beauty are the typical traits of the light, which are obtained by working with the energy which prevails during this day; in the shadow, the expression is of hatred, debauchery and lust.

TEST TO CONFIRM YOU HAVE LEARNED THE LESSON:

- ❖ Feel the positive qualities of this ray by becoming conscious of your breathing at any given moment of the day.

"Love is a synonym for detachment; you only begin to love when you stop needing." Said my sacred voice. *"On the other hand, you begin to unconsciously hate those who you*

need the most. Love is born from freedom, and you are freed only by discipline. You are a slave to your own weaknesses and to those aspects of your life in which you lack discipline." The voice continued as if this time it did not want me to speak. *"The ray of light on this day teaches you to accept yourself without conditions, and to become responsible for your results. Love is born out of eternal acceptance, purpose and service; here is where true love is. Its opposites, like attachment, debauchery, vices and hatred, they are all characteristics of this day as well. When the quality of your thoughts improves, the color of your auric field tends to be clear pink and more subtle; when the contrary happens, it denotes an intense red tint.*

"How come Mars, the God of war, rules this day? I wondered.

"Because the greatest dilemma faced by human beings is that daily struggle, a war, between their purpose and their vices. Breathe in the sacred virtues of this day, so you may liberate yourself from the chains which tie you to the wheel of incarnation; so you may be free; so you may gain the great battle or what Paul the apostle used to call "the good fight;" so you may conquer your inner battles and become conscious of the power behind every decision that you make."

Something inside of me invited me to stay quiet and just observe. We continued, and in front of me, there was a new angel, but this time it was white. I knew it was time to continue.

FORTY EIGHTH RUNE
FOURTH DAY

- Wednesday. Major influence from the planet Mercury.
- Color White.
- Archangel Gabriel.
- Elohim of Purity, known in mythology as the Goddess of light, she creates all the elementals of this day.
- Ascended Master Serapis Bey, one of the masters in charge of the spiritual evolution of planet Earth.
- *FA* is the solfeggio syllable which holds the frequency of the energy on this day.
- The beings of light who support the lessons on this day inhabit the Luxor temple in Egypt.
- Creativity, peace, purity, ascension and resurrection, are the qualities of the light, which are obtained by means of working with the prevailing energy of this day; conflict, death, war and evil are typical in the shadow.

TEST TO CONFIRM YOU HAVE LEARNED THE LESSON:

- ❖ Feel the qualities of this ray as you become conscious of your breathing at any given moment of the day.

As I walked to the next rune, I remember that Archangel Gabriel was the one who announced the coming of Jesus to Mary; as a result, I became confused as to which would be the right religion. Who holds the truth? And just as if like reading my thoughts, the higher me immediately answered:

"All and none. Religious leaders are inspired by ascended masters for as long as they are doing it for the right purpose; they – ascended masters – do not discriminate against any one particular religion. In fact, there can be two leaders within the same religion, where one is inspired and the other is not."

"Then how do I know which one is right?" I wondered in confusion.

"When you leave a temple, you must confirm within yourself that you are leaving filled with power, love and self assurance; during the sermon, you must feel that the religious leader speaks to you only, that he focuses always on the greater good and encourages you to keep your faith and follow the light of God, instead of him. Non–inspired leaders are intriguing, create dependency, do not preach love, manipulate with fear and the ignorance of the people, and they ask to be followed."

"Well, the truth is that I would like to speak with the archangels. Why the need for intermediaries? They are the ones who know the most."

"Your eyes would not be able to see their eyes; their light would blind you. Besides, you would never be able to communicate with an archangel, for his language is not the same as yours. They only manifest themselves from the light."

"So, then?" I could not understand,

"You must do everything through your inner self; when you ask to the light of God in which you inhabit, you are communicating with that which is most sacred in the entire universe, and by celestial law, every time a brother asks for help from the light he always receives an answer."

My inner self? Then, who was I talking to? The deep silence that invaded the place was only interrupted by the majestic figure of a green angel resting at the entrance of the next cloister, and he invited me to go inside.

THIRTY NINTH RUNE
FIFTH DAY

- Thursday. Major influence from the planet Jupiter.
- Color Green; all shades of green are predominant on this day.
- Archangel Raphael, considered the heavenly doctor.
- Elohim Cyclopea, known in mythology as the Goddess Vista, the watchful eye who sees everything, she creates all the elementals on this day.
- Ascended Master Hilarion, one of the masters in charge of the spiritual evolution of planet Earth. He was Paul the apostle in one of his incarnation.
- *SOL* is the solfeggio syllable which holds the frequency of the energy of this day.
- The beings of light give their teachings from the temple at the island of Crete in the Mediterranean Sea.
- Health, truth and an affinity for music and the arts are some of the qualities of the light, which are obtained when working with the prevailing energy of this day; sickness, lies and an affinity for the practice of the dark are typical of the shadow.

TEST TO CONFIRM YOU HAVE LEARNED THE LESSON:

- ❖ Feel the qualities of this ray as you become conscious of your breathing throughout the day.

At some point in time, I heard the Virgin Mary was called Mary Celeste by beings dedicated to the study of all the spiritual doctrines, and that her mission is to help with her energies women who are about to give birth so they may withstand one of their supreme tests; that her energy, like the rest of the ascended masters during meditation, completely envelops planet Earth so they – mothers – may accomplish this test.

On my way to the next cloister, I remembered my mother's devotion for the Virgin Mary and the many testimonies that I heard about her miracles during the course of my life. Could it really be that easy, that by simply invoking the light we get the answer that we are looking for?

A bright flash of light blinded my eyes; it came from the beautiful figure of the ruby angel, the same color as the sun at dusk, a mixture between orange, carrot, red and yellow. I was standing in front of the next rune.

FORTIETH RUNE
SIXTH DAY

- Friday. Major influence from the planet Venus.
- Color Golden Ruby, and the shades of ruby are predominant during this day.
- Archangel Uriel.
- Elohim Tranquility or Peace, known in mythology as the goddess of prosperity and trust, she creates all the elementals on this day.
- Ascended master Lady Nada, whose ray of light was previously wielded by Jesus of Nazareth.
- *LA* is the solfeggio syllable with the vibratory frequency of this day.
- The temple from where the beings of light give their teachings is located in Syria.
- Prosperity, trust and patience are the qualities of light which are obtained by working with the energy that prevails on this day. Poverty, lack of trust and impatience are characteristics of the shadow.

TEST TO CONFIRM YOU HAVE LEARNED THE LESSON:

- ❖ Feel the qualities of this ray as you become conscious of your breathing at any given moment of the day.

"Jesus used to wield that ray? What does he do now?" I wondered.

"He is the master of masters, director of the seven rays."

"So Jesus, who used to talk about poverty, used to wield this ray?"

"Yes, he is the most prosperous being to have ever lived upon Earth; he had the ability to multiply bread and fish, and to turn water into wine. When you are capable of doing such things, you will be at a higher level. By then, you will have no need for a check book."

"How come the runes don't tell the history of the ascended masters? I asked.

"It is there, is just that you did not notice it, mainly because many of those names would not mean anything to you."

"Does that mean one day we will all be ascended masters?"

"Exactly, as well as Elohim and archangels."

"I knew about some masters who were an example in life, but still they died. What happened with them?"

"They were simply not ascended masters; they were masters or beings of greater evolution than yours, with a greater capacity to enlighten others and live in the light, but who still needed to complete other experiences in order to ascend."

⚸

Even though all of this issue was very complicated – mainly because of the catholic education I received from my parents, who were educated themselves by nuns and priests – I was willing to accept the information and not reject it, and to fight the stubborn part of me so it would not trap me in the shadow.

When I entered the next rune, I remembered that at each door there was always an angel, so I quickly went in search for this one. There it was, and violet was his color.

FORTY FIRST RUNE
SEVENTH DAY

- Saturday. Major influence from the planet Saturn.
- Color is violet and all its different shades are predominant on this day.
- Archangel Zadkiel.
- Elohim Arturo, known in mythology as the God of transmutation and forgiveness, he creates all the elementals on this day.
- Ascended master Saint Germain. One of his incarnations was as Joseph, the father of Jesus.
- *TI* is the solfeggio syllable with the vibratory frequency of this day.
- Beings of light give their teachings at a temple in Cuba.
- Transmutation, forgiveness, liberation and cleanliness are the qualities of the light which are obtained by working with the prevailing energy of this day; stagnation, resentment and slavery are the expression of the shadow.

TEST TO CONFIRM YOU HAVE LEARNED THE LESSON:

- ❖ Feel the qualities of this ray as you become conscious of your breathing at any given moment of the day.

"You need to learn many things from this ray. Mainly, that this will be the predominant energy for the next two thousand years, just as on previous years it was the sixth ray, whose director was Jesus. The avatar of these new times will be the ascended master Saint Germain."

"There are those who await the return of Christ and are afraid of the imposter or antichrist."

"Master Jesus brought three, very concrete teachings.
- First, that everything can be summarized in loving, and love gives meaning to everything; a very important lesson considering he gave his life as the supreme symbol of love.
- Second, that in God, in the light, in the Father, everything is possible; "go to Father, my Father who is yours," were his words.
- Third, that the Christ energy is the road toward truth and life, and you must look for Christ within your heart. People expect Christ will return and that is not going to happen; the return of Christ happens when each being discovers him inside their heart. To refuse to look for him inside your heart is to be an antichrist."

This was interesting, I thought. *"So, what changes will we see in these new times?"* I asked.

"The age of the Son ends and the age of the Holy Spirit begins. For this reason, the energy of the planet becomes more subtle; its inhabitants must hold much more love in their hearts and focus their work on the self. The focus will be that of I win, you win; truth will be more common at each moment of your life and detachment will

reign as a way of breaking the chains we have created with our vices. Chaos will prevail in each person until they discover they must look for God within their hearts and keep their temples – meaning, their bodies – pure of thought, word and deed. This ray will accelerate the learning processes of humanity, which means that the lessons must be learned faster; when you work with this ray you reap what you sow quicker."

"Is this is called being born without karma?"

"If you did not have karma you would not be born or die, you would ascend and would be a light master. Thanks to the violet flame, you are going to reap even quicker many of the things you have done, whether you remember them or not."

⸎

I went out on the road after this last answer, and I saw a light and a landscape so infinitely beautiful that I did not want to continue; I sensed nature was celebrating something. I wondered if every deceased person makes it to these runes, and if one could chose to stay, depending on one's level of evolution, in just a few of them. I felt a bit ashamed of myself when I recognized a certain degree of vanity within my thoughts, which only invited to brag, so I just chose to become part of the celebration and enjoy the moment. I began to dance and hum some songs I remembered, as well as some great classical masterpieces and celestial choirs, completely ignoring how they were coming through me; the most amazing thing was the level of pleasure I felt when I sang Handel's Alleluia, a song I knew I had not learned before.

In a delicate and imperceptible way, the celebration brought me to stand in front of a beautiful rainbow which was being guarded by seven majestic, vibrantly colored angels, and each one of them corresponded to a specific ray of light from the cloisters where I had been to. It seemed as if the sign had a magnet leading me magically and unquestionably to the next rune.

RUNE FORTY SECOND
TO WORK IN THE LIGHT

- To live in the light or the shadow is a choice which must be renewed every day.
- Your first thought and feeling, your first word and action of the day must be in the light.
- If you choose to live each new day in the light, manifest it.
- The light is present in your life.
- Invoke the light with the certainty that by law of the universe, you will always get an answer.
- The light cannot be made manifest if it is not first invoked, because you must respect the law of free will, meaning, the capacity to choose your own lessons and the way to learn them.

TEST TO CONFIRM YOU HAVE LEARNED THE LESSON:

DAILY STEPS TO LIVE IN THE LIGHT

- ❖ Connect with your breathing without forcing it, just feel it. Close your eyes and feel how you breathe in the air through your nostrils.

❖ Feel your heart and its beating, and visualize a violet light coming from its center which has the capacity to cleanse your physical body; feel how this light goes all over your body, from head to toe; imagine it surrounds your energy fields and it will clean them and change the frequency of anything that is out of balance in your physical, mental and spiritual auras. Lastly, surround the place where you are with the violet light, and feel how everything is completely clean. Be grateful with all the beings of light who accompany you through this process, because whether you see them or not, there they are. When you invoke the light, there is a legion of angels who come to your side, and if you thank them for their presence without even seeing them, it will be an exemplary show of faith, belief and conviction.

❖ Go back to your heart and pull the sky blue light from its center; imagine that it spreads like a globe all around you and it will protect you from anything unbalanced that tries to come your way, or that you carry within.
  - Make three triangles; one of them has sides which encompass from the top of your head down to your left shoulder, from there to your right shoulder and back to the top of your head again; another one goes from your throat to the left side of your hip, from there to the right side of the hip and back up to your throat; and a third triangle that encompasses from the top of your head to your left foot, from there to the right foot and back up to the top of your head.

  - Finally, imagine the place where you are is totally protected by a blue ray, and again, give thanks to the angels for this ray and for being present with their support.

❖ Invoke the light of the Holy Spirit. Say: "I invoke the light of the Holy Spirit to be made present right here and right now, and so all that I think, feel, speak, do and everything I feed myself on this day, will be for the greater good and the highest of purpose!" Imagine how a white light comes from way above and it goes within you, it envelops you and the place where you are. Then, give sincere thanks and the power of this phrase will stay with you throughout the day, keeping you in a continuous state of creation in alignment with what is recorded in your divine plan."

❖ Go back to your heart and visualize a sun within it, a midday sun, and recognize that as you place your attention in it, there is an activation of the Christ energy in your life, the road to truth and life. Give thanks to the Christ inhabiting within you and declare your decision to keep it alive in your heart. With this, you will gain a clearer understanding of the voice of your heart, which is the voice of God.

❖ Visualize a flame–like light at the center of your heart, and you can rest assured that when you look at it you are looking at God. Talk to it with all your love, with the conviction that, to Him, everything is possible, without time or spatial limits, and everything you ask for with faith you will receive. Follow these four steps:
- First, surrender to Him saying, 'Lord, here I am with all that I am, all I have accomplished and all that I have damaged, with nothing in between us".

- Second, give thanks for everything, the new day, your physical body, your home, and make manifest your intention to live your life with purpose, and any wish you have will be subordinated to the will of God.

- Third, ask with clarity, formulate exactly what you desire and with the certainty that your prayers are heard, and so, they will become true at the right moment and the right place, by grace and in a perfect way.

- And lastly, give thanks to the Father for having heard you, and the more you give thanks, the more clarity you will have with regards to your blessings, as a result of it, you will know they have already been given.

"You have to be clear about the fact that, just as you turn on a lamp in order to get light and sometimes there will be some bugs or insects attracted to it, so it happens when you turn on the light in your life; entities of lesser evolution may come to you in order to feed off of you and rob you of your energies. This will cease to happen when your light is so intense that they will not dare to come close to you, because they will just disintegrate.

"Are you trying to scare me?" I asked my inner voice.

"No. You must know that once you embark upon the road toward the light there is no coming back, even if at times you choose to work from the shadow, in which cases chaos will reign in your life in order to steer you back to the light."

I looked back and I was taken by my fears, anguish, sickness, poverty. I felt pressure in my chest and I could not breathe; depression, a tremendous sense of despair and feelings of wanting to run away invaded my whole being. All of sudden, a while light surrounded me and all of these emotions disappeared. Maybe my internal being wanted to show me the emotions which take over us when we choose to move away from the light and enter our shadow.

"That is the shadow that I refer to," Said my inner being, as if guessing my thoughts, *"to all of what keeps you trapped in the Maya of illusion. It makes you weak and dependent, and it leads you to believe you are not responsible for the results, that you are just the victim of something external. I know at some moments you are the victim of your own self and of your ignorance, and this is what this cloister is about, it is immersing yourself in the wonderful world of the light, or what some call the white magic."*

"When should we invoke the light?" I wondered.

"All human beings have asked themselves the same question. With a bit of awareness you would know. Life is continually renewed, which is why you should be in the light at all moments of your life. Just as nature renews itself every day, so you must renew your intention to live in the light, which you may do with every major choice in your life, and renew – every day – your commitment to live in the light so that the light will intensify even more.

"We have so many blessings, yet we barely use them! We waste them because we ignore their existence."

"Yes, and there are even more blessings. You may work with whatever ray you desire, on the day of your choice; in order to do this, you must fill yourself with the light of a specific ray and invoke it with certainty: "I invoke the light of prosperity so that money may flow into my life constantly, abundantly and legally" or "I invoke the light of health so that my body may live healthy, young, graceful and vigorous" and so it will be done. In both cases, your energetic fields will be filled with the appropriate colors and frequency. Another way to do it is by visualizing yourself inside this specific ray of light, and at night before you go to bed, ask to be guided to the temple of light which corresponds to that day, so you may learn everything you need to know about the ray; and so it will be. Even though you may not remember anything the next morning, you must trust you were in fact at the temple, and that you were filled with its energy. Then, the magic of life – what sometimes is called a coincidence – will begin to surround and surprise you day after day.

I could only conclude that in order to learn, apply, grow and change, I had also run out of time. When I got to the next rune, I stopped at the door in order to look at the color of the angel, but I noticed this particular cloister had no angel, or at least not one within my range of sight. I went in slowly, and realized that many of the previous runes did not have an angel either.

FORTY THIRD RUNE
THE NEW AGE

- The New Age is the age if light, love, faith, wisdom, prosperity and power.
- It is the age of the Holy Spirit.
- It is the times in which *leading by example* will be the norm and the power of fraud will decay.
- In these times you must live by the premise "I win, you win" and in excellence.
- Human improvement will focus in the Being and in things, which lasts, like humility, perseverance, honesty, tolerance and uniformity.
- This is an age when it will be evident that only discipline makes you free, and being a libertine enslaves you.
- In the New Age, you must live within your purpose and in service, and recognize that the road must be guided by divine light.
- Being an example will not be the most important aspect, but it will be the only important aspect.
- People will work to benefit themselves, their families, their work, the society in which they live and the planet in general. It will be a completely ecologically oriented society.
- Those religions, which invite their followers to practice what, it preaches, and whose leaders are en example of light, will be the only ones to survive.
- Companies will have to operate with the purpose of benefiting its owners, employees, clients and the environment.

- Anything obscure will be revealed to the public, because nothing can be hidden when you live in the light.
- In the New Age – considered the age of uncovering – you need to act, think, speak and feel knowing that everything you do, think, speak and feel will be publicly available to all, because this is how it will be.
- Human beings will understand their power and become responsible for it, choosing to live in the light of Christ.
- It will be a time of change and chaos, until each being finds the light of God within their heart, and understands and accepts that he is conditioned by the natural laws with which he needs to be in alignment.
- When the New Age begins, there will be a proliferation of religions; however, in the end, there will only be left those which are based in the light, love and the power that all human beings carry within their hearts.
- The New Age is not a religion. It is a new life style whose predominant thought is the greater good.
- There will be Christians of the old and of the new age, just as Catholics, Mohammedans, Jehovah's Witnesses, and followers of the other religions; the difference will be that in the New Age the practice will be made by example.
- There will be so many changes, on all aspects, during the New Age that it will be difficult to believe we could have lived without the availability of the new technology. There will be almost inevitable, radical changes which will happen every twenty years over the course of the first one hundred years.
- The world's problems and chaos can be explained in the sense that the planet is getting ready for new times; a transition which will be completed once its

inhabitants choose to change in their lives everything contrary to love. To make or not this conscious choice will be a temporary measure, for in the end the universe will inevitably take us there.

A new era where love and light will reign is the compulsory change of these new times. Whoever is not prepared and does not transition voluntarily, will find himself riddled with his own internal battles in order to be undoubtedly lead to change.

TEST TO CONFIRM YOU HAVE LEARNED THE LESSON:

❖ Lead by example.

"I was so mistaken with regards to the New Age! I thought it was something demonic, a new religion of libertines, black magic, amulets and a bunch of fake stuff, and I also thought they were guided by the antichrist."

"The New Age is a change on all aspects of life on Earth." Explained my sacred, inner voice.

"Like what?" I asked.

"Ruptures. Anything you are tied to or you depend on will be taken from you and you will be invited to enter into a greater state of consciousness with regards to trust and freedom, which can happen –for example– with relationship to work, your couple, finances or vices."

"Should I assume then that break ups are welcomed? And the end of marriages and going broke in business?"

"That rigidity of thought only blocks your understanding. Understand that everything which limits or stagnates your growth will be removed from your life. If your love

relationship is based on love and mutual respect, if each one lives within their purpose and neither one is a block on the road to the other's evolution, then that relationship will last for a long time. If you work out of fear of not having, and you feel you are not putting all of your gifts to the service of humanity, then for sure your will lose that job; on the contrary, if you feel full with what you do and you live the greater good through your work, then you will know that if that job is over is because the universe is preparing something even greater for you. If the vision of your business is excellence and service for the benefit of your employees, associates, clients and the planet in general, then with each day you will become more prosperous. Remember, in this age people will live in trust based on the knowledge of two fundamental things, that everything happens for your greater good and anything is possible."

This was quite the explanation. However, I still asked, "Everything that enslaves me, makes me stagnant or limits me, will leave my reality?

"Yes, just as anything which makes you dependent and attached."

"One generally creates dependency with one's children, so does that mean I must part from them?" I was puzzled.

"Live in freedom, this means, with discipline and without attachment. Recognize that you only own the lessons you learn along the road, and everything else is just borrowed, be that your parents, children, work and material belongings. If you watch carefully, you will discover that the areas of your life in which there is no discipline keep you enslaved. So make sure you constantly enjoy everything, without becoming attached to anything, and as a result, you will eradicate all pain from your life. I will illustrate by telling you a story. Once upon a time there was a lady who had four

children, and the oldest one died when he was only twenty one years old; during the memorial, she told her other children – who cried for the death of their brother – that instead of crying and complaining for his parting, to learn to be grateful and invited them to say the following prayer with her: 'Lord, You, Creator of the heaven and the earth, You, who knows the real reason behind all things, you have decided that my beloved son should return to your side, and as it is your will, I accept it. I take this moment to thank you for having allowed me to have him for twenty–one years. Amen.' After that, the whole place was in silence and all the crying stopped; they remembered, how we must always do, that there is nothing in the entire universe which moves without it being the will of God."

"What is, in summary, the best definition of the New Age? I wondered.

"It is an age of rebirth during which the greater good will reign, as well as discernment, leading by example and the confirmation of the unlimited power of human beings, who thanks to their close relationship to God and an unwavering confidence in His guidance, will create ever better and easier ways to do things based on love of self, of others and of their labor."

ƒ

I would have liked to be on Earth, for these new changes sounded very promising. I focused on the movements of my body and I felt very light; the sound of the contact of my feet with the air made me happy. How much did I still have to learn? *Everything about eternity* was the immediate answer.

"The last runes have to do with the newest teachings, and because it is such novel information you will need more time in order to properly understand them."

"How new can these runes be for me?"

"They are the ones which you have not repeated, even though you have worked on them. In your last third dimensional life, you delved deeper in their knowledge, and you were preparing to reach a higher level of wisdom of each one of them. These subjects seem new to you, like when you learned algebra and you already had basic math knowledge."

"Does that mean I had already seen the previous ones?" The previous runes, I meant.

"Yes, your learning process with the previous runes encompasses several life times, and some of them more than you can even imagine. The subjects of which you have a better grip of are those you have worked with the most and that have been the easiest to understand. The scholar has simply dedicated a lot of time to the work; in some cases it takes several lives learning the same and acquiring various experiences in relationship to the subject in order to bring the person to a higher level of mastership of it."

"Is that where genius kids come from?

"Yes. Before they were born, Mozart and Beethoven were beings who dedicated several previous life times to the study and learning of music."

"What about me? Will I ever be a great musician?"

"Exactly, you will be 'a great' on all aspects of human wisdom.

I kept feeling more and more that the art of living and walking toward the light required a greater sense of responsibility than what I could have ever imagined. The important thing was to not feel resented or try to get ahead of myself, for everything would come to me in due time. I recognized I could apply the law of acceptance more easily now, without feelings of guilt.

FORTY FOURTH RUNE
DEATH

- Death is the natural renovation of the physical body.
- You choose your parents, the span of your life, gender, as well as forty–eight runes or subjects to learn which will turn into the purpose of your life.
- You leave the cycle of life and death when all of your creations are in alignment with the natural laws, and when you sow love, wisdom and justice in the light. Then, you will be born, grow up and you will not die, you will ascend. You will become an ascended master.
- Just like at the beginning of your school year you may expect four different outcomes – to end the year and pass all your courses, to end the year and flunk, to be expelled or retire before the school year ends – you can also expect to die of natural causes and accomplish, die of natural causes and not accomplish, die incidentally or commit suicide.
- Although every person, regardless of his life style or type of death, is always in God – is part of God and can never be separate from God – in any of the last three types of death the vibration is so dense that the person cannot perceive their oneness with God. The same happens in life to many people that, even though they are in God, they mentally disconnect themselves from Him and refuse to perceive Him.
- A natural death coupled with the accomplishment of your purpose is a full and wonderful experience. It is a face to face reunion with the Creator and with those who died before you, an analysis of what you did coming

from a state of fullness and the conscious selection of both new subjects of study, as well as your new set of parents, life span in the third dimension, gender and a new set of forty eight runes or lessons. Those who by their degree of evolution are prepared for this type of death will not be afraid of it, and will be able to predict the moment when it shall pass.

- A natural death with no accomplishment of the purpose is the kind of death for those who spend most of their lives living outside of their purpose. They experience death as someone who surrenders to an event without desiring it and with the feeling that they have no other choice. It is a reunion with the self and his consciousness, and with those who died of natural cause and did not accomplish either. From the regret, they analyze how they acted and make a conscious decision to repeat the lessons they need to learn; they select parents, the same life span in the third dimension, the same gender and the same forty–eight runes. These are not prepared for this type of death, and as such, they are afraid of it and cannot foresee it.
- Incidental death is that in which the person died without wanting to, before he was able to finish the life span he had chosen to live. It is an unconscious choice due to living outside of his purpose and interrupting the evolution of other human beings; it is typical of those who surrender to an experience without accepting it and with the feeling they had no other choice. It is a reunion with the self and his consciousness, as well as those who also had an incidental death and did not accomplish their purpose. They desire to postpone the self–evaluation and remain bound to Earth; however, what was done is inevitably analyzed and they end up feeling sorry; because of this, they make the conscious decision to

repeat the subject of learning; they select parents, the same third dimensional life span, the same gender and the same forty–eight runes. They are not prepared for this type of death, because of that they are afraid of it and cannot accept it or foresee it.

- Death by suicide. To take one's life creates a constant state of repent, the desire for everything to be no more than a dream, coupled with the feeling of not having any other option. It is a face to face reunion with the self and one's unbalances, a continuous state of suffering from which the person cannot find a way out. After much suffering, the process continues from the perspective of repent; then, there is an analysis of how the person acted in life and he makes the conscious decision to repeat the subjects of study and to never again take his life, for which a new set of parents is selected, the life span in the third dimension, gender and forty eight runes. Those who find death this way go through a very tough and painful experience, after which they will never even think about taking their own life and will value every second of their existence.

TEST TO CONFIRM YOU HAVE LEARNED THE LESSON:

- ❖ Live every day as if it was the last one of your existence.

"In life, I met very good people who accidentally died; now it turns out that those who died in such a way was because they were not learning and did not allow others to learn, and because of that they were kicked out of life"

"No, what you are saying is a misinterpretation." Said *my inner voice. "The type of death has nothing to do with the way in which they die, it is only related with the life span*

the person had chosen. For example, if someone selected to live for seventy years in order to learn and fulfill his purpose, and it turns out he dies before that time by his own will, that is a suicide; If he dies not by his own will, then it is an incidental death. You will never know what type of death was that of each and every one, this is only known by the one who is dying."

I inferred that to live and die is an opportunity to learn, and I was now going through my own evaluation before going back to select my next runes. I remembered the story of a gentleman who saw death, and when death saw the man's face filled with anguish it simply told him, 'How strange! We had agreed to meet today, but somewhere else!' Next thing you know, the man ran away from the site and went back to his hometown; once at his parents' home, he went into his room and laid down on his bed, which he felt was more comfortable than ever. Death showed up again in his room and said, 'Now this is where we were supposed to meet!' And just as he said, the gentleman died.

I speculate one cannot be born or die a day before or after, so I do not understand how come I ran out of time on Earth on that precise day; I feel it is unfair that we are not told beforehand about something so transcendental. Or maybe we are given notice but we lack the sensitivity to perceive the signs the universe is giving, and we cannot understand its language?

I was followed to the next rune by a sense of doubt. What type of death was mine? A chill went up and down my spine and I decided to ignore the answer, all I did was pick up my pace and listen to the sound of the wind, which was very distracting at the moment. Fortunately, I was already in front of my next lesson.

FORTY FIFTH RUNE
TWIN SOULS

- Yin and yang, negative and positive, feminine and masculine are all parts of a whole called *the atom*.
- In essence, that atom is love, justice and wisdom.
- The yin and yang separate in order to begin the process of self–knowledge and each one of those parts is what you know with the name of Higher Self.
- When you ask for the light, you may invoke the part or the counterpart, Father God and Mother God.
- In the evolutionary process, and in some of your lives, you may find that being whose light is the counterpart of your inner self or higher self. These two parts of the same spark of light are called twin souls.
- In some lives, it is not necessary to encounter your twin soul, but searching for it teaches you to give unconditional love.
- The reunion with a twin soul may happen after many lives, in which case they are the ideal couple to be with in a romantic relationship, or it can even be a short, yet very intense relationship that supports your further evolution.
- When you find your twin soul, your heart knows it without interpretation or need for validation, it just knows.
- One day, after having learned much, you will know exactly where your twin soul is and who it is.
- After your ascension as a master of light, you will reunite again with your twin soul and will merge with

it forever, and that is when the mandate will be fulfilled: 'what God has joined together, let no man separate'.

TEST TO CONFIRM YOU HAVE LEARNED THE LESSON:

- Clean your energetic fields with the violet flame.

- Protect yourself with the blue flame.

- Ask the light of the Holy Spirit for the greater good and the highest of ends.

- Visualize the Christ energy in your heart.

- Visualize the light as the flame of a candle, at the center of your heart; it expresses your superior self.

- Invoke the essence of your twin soul, wherever it is, so it will make itself present at that place and time where you are. Visualize its light in front of you and create a bridge of rose–colored light, the light of love. Let this light go out from your heart and reach the heart of your twin soul!

- Speak to your twin soul. Make your feelings known to it; then, you may say good–bye and tell it that when the time is right, as well as the place, you will meet again.

Always diligent – I thought to myself – my higher self–made it clear to me that this simple exercise helps me to be free to share with other partners and to close my emotional cycles without leaving behind any kind of karmic attachment.

I wonder where my twin soul is at this moment? What kind of experiences is she having and what are her lessons? Sometime ago I read there are lives in which we are so mean, aggressive and atrocious that our twin soul decides to leave our side and wait another period in order to be with us.

Wanting to learn more about my twin soul, I chose to leave this journey of continuous learning and step aside for a while in this nirvana or paradise, and I found a beautiful place to do it. I sat down in the middle of a multicolored garden, on a stone which seemed to have been designed for meditation purposes. There, I practiced the exercise I had just read in the rune and I felt I really was in front of her, my twin soul; I said so many things and I heard so many more that I cannot even consider that it could have been some trick from my imagination; maybe the law of synchronicity allowed us to unite in our eternity in order to share this magical moment.

As I walked, I thought about the promise we had just made to each other during the meditation, so our reunion would be happening very soon. My heart started to race and I felt butterflies in my stomach; feelings like those of a teenager in love surged from within the deepest parts of my being.

FORTY SIXTH RUNE
PHYSICAL IMMORTALITY

- You never die; you only change body or vehicle.
- The best that you have ever been and the worst you can be is what you are today.
- You come from ignoring who you really are, and you are moving toward the complete and total understanding and knowledge of yourself, toward wisdom, toward your light.
- Everything is in evolution; everything is constantly getting better, even when you cannot perceive it and your internal judgment makes you think otherwise.
- It is fair that every atom which makes up the whole should go with the flow of its own evolution or self-knowledge.
- For the Creator of life, it is no better or worse that someone is in higher or lower levels of learning; to Him, everyone is an apprentice.
- To live or die is a choice made at higher levels of consciousness.
- You are trapped in the cycles of life and death until everything you sowed gets balanced.
- You will harvest everything as a result of every thought, word and deed you might have sowed during all of your lives, and when you are done harvesting, you will become an ascended master.
- Ascended master is the one who became responsible for all of his creations and today chooses to sow only in the light. He is born and grows, does not reproduce or get old, only transcends; no one ever sees him die,

and from this moment on, his mission is to guide his brothers of lesser evolution toward the light.
- The need or the obligation to die is a line of thinking you have not allowed yourself to question.
- Whatever you believe, that is what is. If you think death is inevitable, your body will support you unconditionally and it will produce sickness, old age and death.
- Physical immortality invites you to be happy with your existence in a responsible way.

TEST TO CONFIRM YOU HAVE LEARNED THE LESSON:

❖ See life as an infinite game, where everything you sow will be harvested in God's time, which is always perfect.

"What is the purpose of dying and being born again, over and over, if we cannot remember anything we have lived before? Maybe is best to be physically immortal."

"You remember the lesson but not word by word. Just as you know how to add, you do not remember the specific exercises with which you were taught."

"Does that mean I already learned not to kill?"

"Exactly, and you did so by taking other people's opportunities to learn and from seeing how you yourself were robbed of it as well, until one day you got bored of that vicious circle and you changed what you sowed."

"If one chooses parents, gender, lessons and life span, what is the purpose of living if everything is already pre–determined?"

"You are the creator of your own movie called Life. You chose your parents, what you needed to learn in life and the examples with which you learned; you yourself limited or expanded your learning process out of your own accord. When you went to college you knew which courses you were taking, however, what gave purpose to studying was exactly what you were going to learn in class. Life is the same way."

"Could we make mistakes that we did not make before? Meaning, is there such thing as involution?"

"No. There is not. Once you learn a lesson, the learning is recorded forever. Nonetheless, the law of reversibility verifies that you do not make it to the next level of knowledge until you have completed the previous one, and if you make new mistakes you will be facing new lessons."

"And is it possible to have been rich before and now poor, or a woman previously and now a man?"

"Yes, because if there was only one life to live there would be no justice. Some would be privileged and others would not, so the blind and the not blind, the woman and the man, the rich and the poor, the healthy and the sick, would not have access to the same opportunities to experiment. Eternal things remains; in other words, if you accumulated money out of your fear to be poor, you may choose to live without it in another life; but if you already learned how to live in prosperity, that is something which will forever belong to you. If you work in life on your inner self, your lessons learned will remain; you will be able to create again, you will surpass your previous results and the quality of your life will continuously improve, because to master a subject is a synonym for evolution. Remember, it is about mastering, no depending. On the contrary, whatever

you do in relationship to doing and having will disappear at the moment of your death."

"Are you saying one day we will all be beings of light? Ascended masters?"

"Exactly, although by then there will be new students in the lower levels of learning, and probably thousands of millions of years would have passed."

⚜

Remaining silent was a good decision, for reflecting helped me to internalize the lessons from the runes and the dialogues with my inner sacred being, which confronted me and forced me to dedicate sometime after each rune to ponder about the subject. Conscious of everything I had been told, logically, I decided to continue to the next cloister, not without first marveling at the magnificence of this place of beautiful landscapes and sounds of silence, because even though it may seem like a paradox, they were sounds of silence. I wondered why I was rushing through this place that was so perfect in every way. Is it that I am going somewhere else? I slowed down my pace and I found myself standing in front of my next lesson.

FORTY SEVENTH RUNE
THE POWER OF LOVE

- Love is the result of acceptance, purpose and service.
- Only love gives sense to your existence. Love both the moment when you sow, and the moment when you reap.
- The power of love takes you away from the world inhabited by the living dead, those who live with anguish in their hearts because they have fallen prey to the illusion of competition.
- You will be able to manifest true love through the purity of your own heart.
- Love your brothers and sisters as you love yourself. Hence, first love yourself, because no one can give what he or she does not have.
- The moment to love is the present. Live every moment of your existence with love.
- Whatever you do, do it with love or do not do it.
- Hate is the result of rejection, vice and selfishness; do not allow those viruses to take over your heart.
- Love unconditionally. Just as The One who created you did not impose any kind of conditions in order to do it.
- Love is a synonym for freedom. Free yourself from everything that enslaves you.
- You will continue to run into the people you reject until you learn to love them.
- When you close cycles your energy levels will increase, and the best way to do it is through love.
- All lessons can be summarized in *just love*.

- You begin to love someone when you stop needing them.
- You unconsciously reject those who need you the most.
- To love is different from falling in love.
- You love when you give anything without expecting anything in return.
- You fall in love when you share time, space, problems and admiration.
- Love all of your past, your memories, the experience you have lived, your disenchantments, your successes, your failures, your days of solitude and the ones with company, your days of prosperity and the days of lack. Besides loving your past, the only other possibility is to learn from it.
- When is it late to love? When you do not love in the present moment, because it will never come back.

TEST TO CONFIRM YOU HAVE LEARNED THE LESSON:

❖ Love unconditionally.

My first and most rushed conclusion was that I had fallen in love many times, but I had rarely loved.

I remembered a beautiful time of my life. There were multicolored landscapes and sensations of wellbeing, fullness and joy...Yes, I was in love; everything was rose-colored. All of a sudden, everything about my existence made sense; I left the monotony and embarked upon the beautiful experience of living. She was a woman whose face reflected the conclusion of the world in an instant; so tender, so human, so complete within herself that everything a man could have dreamed of about a woman, she was.

Our encounter was in reality a reunion; I felt, in the deepest reaches of my being, I had met her on some previous lives. Her sweet face reflected the dawn of the day; her presence made me tremble, butterflies fluttered inside my stomach and my whole body shook. Her voice resounded in my mind with messages from beyond, prophetic feelings and invitations to trust that I was indeed awakening to a new experience, one filled with happiness and that I had to live, for it was written in the book of life.

It was easy to begin a conversation, as it usually happens when two people reunite after having been apart for a long time, and in the midst of the reunion there is the need to tell one another up to the last little detail of everything that happened since the last time you saw each other. There was no doubt; I knew beyond the limits of time and space that I already knew her, even though I did not know when or where we had met, or at what point of my eternal existence.

Through her, I learned to love, to discover and embrace the formula which expresses the love between a couple, to share time, space and even some problems, with a high dosage of admiration for the other person. It was interesting to put this formula to the test. For as long as the space is more reduced, you share more time together, there are more problems and you have an even greater sense of admiration for the other person, the love between the two keeps increasing. Couples who do the opposite to this tend to go on a roll of falling out of love. What we had was not only the result of being in love; it was first and foremost about the reunion, which makes a big difference.

We shared a lot. I cherish this part of my life as if it was a fairy tale, which I find it hard to believe I actually lived. We use to cite verses from Jibran: "True love is born right at the moment of the reunion" and we were proud to know this is what had happened to us; like magic, immediate, effortless and without conquering... "If you already had that experience, you will understand," what some people call *love at first sight*. I felt nostalgic. The imminence of the last rune told me I was running out of time and I was questioning whether I could have taken more advantage of it. The thought of it made me feel restless and anxious. I thought that yet again, experiences had come into my life but they came and went in a rush, and maybe I did not take the time to be present at every single place, to enjoy it fully and learn everything that was available to me.

Why did this happen to me? Not even now, dead, am I able to surrender and experience every moment to the fullest? I yelled at the top of my lungs; to suffer or feel guilty, but what for? I must simply surrender to the experience of this process. That was my immediate conclusion upon reflection, as I continued to feel the burning and raspy sensation in my throat.

As I analyze these experiences and what I have lived in this place, I conclude that, to tell you the truth, the lessons of these runes were already known in the third dimension; could it be that creative geniuses are just beings with an excellent memory of the beyond?

A big sign I had already read in life – which was Pythagoras' – silenced my being when I went out of that place:

"You will easily appreciate men who are the creators of their misadventures. In their disgrace, they cannot see the blessings they have in front of them; their ears shut to the truth. How few of them are actually aware of the real medicine for their evils!"

My pace was slow and sad, because I was aware of the imminence of the end. The sign in the last rune caught me by surprise, and at the entrance, colored markers and beings of light welcomed me.

FORTY EIGHTH RUNE
THE SUPREME BLESSINGS

- Blessed be those who love because their hearts will be forever filled with happiness.
- Blessed be those who smile for they will have good health.
- Blessed be the dreamers because they will transform the world.
- Blessed be those who give without expecting anything in return for their price will be multiplied.
- Blessed be the carriers of hope because they will appease the afflictions of the Earth.
- Blessed be those who discover their unlimited power for they will become responsible for what they reap.
- Blessed be those who listen because they learn continuously.
- Blessed be those that discover the power of the light within their hearts because they will eliminate their limitations.
- Blessed be the ones who serve because they are the hands of God on Earth.
- Blessed be the honest ones for they live in the light.
- Blessed be the ones who take advantage of every second of their life for they will be very prosperous.

- Blessed be the ones who pray because they will be heard and their requests will be met.
- Blessed be the ones who meditate because they will hear God.
- Blessed be those who practice contemplation for they will see the face of God.
- Blessed be those who practice spiritual exercises because they will be united with God.
- Blessed be the ones who see the face of God in every human being for they will be blessed with the gift of wisdom.
- Blessed be those who are willing to conquer their own battles because they will be examples of life.

The only thing I did not like in this cloister was that I could not read the blessings given by the master Jesus Christ; I do not know why, but somehow I concluded that these blessings were my own creations, fruit of the lessons learned by going through the previous runes. I determined we all finish a stage of our learning process by writing our own blessings, though I did not know at what moment I did so. Once I was outside of the cloister and gave back the markers, I noticed I had actually used them.

PART V

ENLIGHTENMENT

I was tired of pondering, learning and clarifying so many subjects. Nonetheless, it was clear to me that the learning process is an eternal road, and as such, I was somewhere in my journey and everybody else was in some part of theirs. I understood that as we advance in our comprehension of things, we get tools which help improve the quality of our lives, and no matter how difficult a certain vital cycle may seem, it always moves us forward in our evolutionary process.

I felt in ecstasy as I observed the landscape; to observe without a judgment was a virtue that I seldom practiced. Almost invariably, as soon as I would observe something, a judgment of some sort would come to the surface, but this time it did not happen.

There were many people; each one lived in his own world experiencing his own processes. Even though we were so diverse, we were part of the same all and the separation was only mental.

I knew I had to say goodbye to this place and begin and new journey, or a new life, which made me consider that all the experience I had just had going through these runes did make sense, and as such, it was my time. Again, my guardian angel, God, the voice of my consciousness, the perfected part of me, was guiding me.

END OF THE DIALOGUES

"The only way you are going to corroborate whether you learned your lessons or not is by subjecting yourself to a test, and for that, it is important that you go through another vital period in the third dimension. It is there where you will be able to verify the reality of what you have learned."

I was surprised to hear this. "Do you mean I have to be born again, live and die?"

"Exactly!" said my inner voice.

"It does not make sense! I guess I read as much as I needed and as a result I have learned what I needed to learn about those runes."

"To read is not the same as to learn. Only applied knowledge can persist in your spirit, so it is time for you to practice the information you have received."

"I must repeat?" I asked.

"In reality you never repeat. You will change what you sow and as a result your harvest will change; you will attract new people into your life and you will live new experiences. The way you respond to them and your capacity to sow better crops will determine how much you learned."

"Does that mean I can choose what I need to learn in my next vital cycle?"

"You already did during the final cloister. Now you must continue, with what you learned you made ready your next lessons."

"And what will be my purpose? Will it be the same?"

"Your purpose changes as the lessons you need to learn change. For example, if you need to intensify the learning of being of service, then your purpose will be oriented toward that; if your main subject to learn has to do with discovering your power, then maybe your creativity will never be an important part of your purpose. What is most important is that you know that it is never the same; even more, there are multiple levels to learn the same lesson. Remember, the learning process is infinite."

"What must I do now in order to continue?" I wondered.

"It is easy. The eternal quality of your being is recorded in your history. Are you ready?"

"Yes" I answered.

"So, leave it all and follow me."

"What do you mean? Leave what?"

"I mean your past. You will become a new being."

We walked through a paradise of ineffable beauty. Any word would be insufficient in order to describe such wonder. Everything in that place was perfection, and it shone with a light of its own. I felt moved when I realized I doing so as well. A sun was being projected from the center of my chest, it was the closest I knew to the Christ energy, what Jesus Christ had spoken about on Earth, which is the way toward truth and life.

I noticed that each person had his own level of higher or lower intensity of light emanated by that sun, and this was a sign of the different level of evolution for each being. The more evolved the being was, the more brilliant the light was; the lesser the evolution, the lesser the light.

Our life's experiences make us the bearers of either a greater or lesser light of our Christ energy, and because of this, we enjoy a greater or lesser degree of communication with our internal being.

Jesus said more than two thousand years ago, "I AM THE WAY TOWARD TRUTH AND LIFE," and it was not until now that I was able to understand it, just as I understood the words, "Look for Christ inside your heart." The more evolved a person is, the brighter the sun within their hearts, his Christ energy and his connection to God are even greater.

By being more connected to God, we are also more connected with our purpose and our life cycle becomes more enjoyable. In reality, we all have that connection, even though some have a greater capacity to hear what is essential, which is a capacity they have earned with the lessons they learned from one life to another. Besides, people whose success is worthy of being copied have a strong belief in God, and they are in close communication with Him regardless of the religion they profess.

Life's journey is a return from the world of matter to our essence through a process of continuous learning, until the day our will is at the mercy of our creator. From that moment on, our road will be filled with happiness, fullness and gratitude for each experience lived, no matter whether it may be qualified as good or bad. On the contrary, the less evolved a person is, the greater the level of mental separation from God. It is an irony that at that stage of evolution people tend to look for God outside of themselves, and the disconnection from their own internal being is such that they feel depressed, bored and as if life has no meaning, which makes it easy to seek refuge in vice.

I looked at my heart and the more attention I paid to my Christ energy, the greater my sensation of joy, fullness and happiness. I felt I was eternity and I was proud of myself, and before I even began to judge my pride, I was able to see the light inside of me. Caught by surprise, thinking it was some sort of optical illusion, I decided to seek God outside of me again, around me, but He was not there. This time, instead of feeling sad, I felt even happier, because I immediately understood that the only place where I could seek and find him, for the rest of my eternity, would be inside my own heart. Feeling grateful, I outlined a summary of what I had learned:

1. I must be grateful for all my experiences, regardless of whether I believe they are good or bad; beyond the Maya of illusion of suffering and enjoyment, I know there is a lesson to learn from everything.

2. In the journey of my life, I can only find the right answers inside of me.

3. The universe always listens to and supports the materialization of the most authentic desires of my heart.

4. The God in which I inhabit has no limits, hence, I am unlimited.

5. The only condition for our wishes to come true is that they be made for the greater good. Like in the tale of Aladdin's Lamp, the lamp is my heart, the genie is God, and I am the master and creator of my wishes.

6. We must go back a thousand times to the silence of the heart, because there is where the right answers lie.

7. In times of unrest, despair, lack of hope and confusion, I must remember I do not need to fight against life; on the contrary, I must connect with life and let everything flow from the light of my heart.

I wished to remain in the repetition of what I had learned so that it would never be erased from my memory, but my higher self took me away from such illusion.

"It is time to continue with your preparations." He said.

I went into another grand movie theater where there were angels and beings of light with faces that reflected purity. I sat on a big couch, and immediately, a projection of the movies of my lives was shown on the screen in front of me.

There were many feelings I experienced at that moment. Sadness, nostalgia for the past moments and people who came back to my mind; it seemed as if both them and the experiences themselves were present right there and now with me. I was surprised to see many absurdities, for example, when I found out what I had been, and to see myself in the body of a woman; for loving intensely a person whom I had hurt before; for reaping a harvest of something which I had sowed on a previous life, without even understanding it; for seeing all of these and understanding that everything I have lived throughout my eternity is perfect and fair.

I knew which would be the subjects I would have to repeat and which ones would be new; I knew, but without a complete understanding, what would be the main purpose of my next life. However, when I asked if I could hear it once more, the only answer I received was the following:

GO BACK TO YOUR HEART AGAIN AND AGAIN, BECAUSE THE INFORMATION ABOUT YOUR PURPOSE AND HOW TO ACCOMPLISH IT IS IN THERE.

Then, I lived a process where I integrated my mind with my new forty-eight seals and during which I determined the amount of time I was going to live this time, my gender and my parents. I selected them from within the pool of people with whom I had shared previous lives and with whom I still had some unfinished karmic ties.

Lastly, a blinding ray of light followed by a profound darkness overtook me, and I was transported to a place of fog...I think I died again.

REBIRTH

Now I am in a place where I feel comfortable and with a nice temperature; I am about to arrive I do not know where. Everything is magical.

Who am I, where do I come from, where am I, where am I going? It does not matter, everything here is plentiful and I have lived here for a long time.

What is happening? Why so much noise? Who moans? I do not understand why I am being forced to leave! This is incomprehensible; I am in a very tight place and I am being mistreated. How cold! That light is blinding me! And something hurts my skin. Why are they spanking me? I am going to cry.

Again, everything is happiness and I do not understand why. I could swear that whoever is feeding me with her breast is someone I already knew; besides the fact I was inside her womb, I have this feeling that I know her from before. Yes, I have a feeling that once I lived with her for a long time without expressing my feelings toward her; I do not know when this was, but that is how it happened; she left my life without me having the opportunity to express the love I always felt for her; this experience taught me one can only love in the present moment, and on that occasion it became late for me to love her.

WAKING UP

If God gives you one more day to live, enjoy it to the fullest and live it with intensity, it is best to live tired rather than frustrated. Give thanks to the heavens and bless the world with your actions. A long time ago, Seneca taught that it is not that we have a short time to live, but it is that we waste too much of it.

* * *

Somebody shook me with force and I woke up abruptly. When I opened my eyes, there she was in front of me; her long hair partially covering her angelic face and her brown colored eyes. Her penetrating gaze filled with love and understanding told me that it was time to go back to sleep.

"Now this time it has gotten really late; it has been a long time since you take such a long siesta," she said as she woke me up.

I was astonished by the lucid dream I had just had. It was a moment of complete introspection; I remembered everything so clearly that I promised myself I would write it.

I went over the whole situation again. I considered my feelings before I fell asleep, the permanent state of exhaustion and the exaggerated tiredness produced by the unfinished business and the cycles to close, the decision to jump into action, the choice to live fully in the present and live it without condition so that I would not have to regret it later on; so that I would not have to arrive to the conclusion that it was too late to love because in the present is already too late to love what was not loved in its moment.

I made sure to remember the main lessons from the dream: that the moment of power and love is the present; that I am in God, and having a good communication with Him facilitates our transit through life; I have been created with a purpose or life plan and with the appropriate gifts to make it true; the world obeys the natural laws which, whether we know them or not, they work and condition our lives; I have five great powers to change the world, which are, the power of imagination, the verb, the action, the feelings and the food; I need to continuously choose between living in the light or the darkness; and the most important thing is that to self–impose limits is an expression of our ignorance.

I wanted to recapitulate properly every message from this dream so that I could relay them in a neutral and thorough manner, without conditioning them with my beliefs and internal paradigms. It seemed as if I was being asked to, maybe, convey a revelation? Either way, it was decided; this experience needed to be told around the world, maybe through a book, and so I would, despite the fact that many of the subjects I would have to cover were new to me.

When I noticed I was making a new promise to myself, I connected with the aversion to having unfinished business that I had felt just before the siesta, and with the urgent need to spring into action. So, I jumped and sat down in the sofa; the clock signaled it was 2:20 in the afternoon. I had slept for over an hour; I could not continue with this habit if I was serious about changing the results of my life, if I really desired to act immediately and unwaveringly in order to accomplish all of my unfinished business.

I took a deep breath and promised myself I would sprang into action. When I got out of the sofa, I felt my body was heavy; I had been accumulating weight for some time now, and every time I thought I would lose it, I would come up with some sort of excuse and end up giving up on my intention.

This time everything would be different. The words 'action, action, action' kept resonating in my mind, as well as 'miracles are made.' I vehemently repeated to myself a phrase I had read on a self–improvement book: "I am going to live until I die, and will not seek to confuse death with life. For as long as I remain on this earth I am resolved to live. Why live half ways?"

I got up ready to complete everything unfinished, like writing a book and losing weight. As I walked diligently toward the study, the pleasing smell of coffee and almond emanated from the kitchen, a voice from the dining room invited me to taste the exquisite flavor of my favorite dessert...And there, I found myself again in front of an apparently dilemma, and at the same time, a profound dilemma.

A NOTE FROM THE AUTHOR

My dearest friend: Do you think this book has provided you with a set of valid tools which will allow you to improve the quality of your life? Did it increase your light? Share it with your friends...

If you wish to participate in one of my workshops or acquire some of our audio, you may contact us via email:
daniel.hernandezx1@gmail.com

Visit us on:
https://www.facebook.com/danielhernandezx1

https://www.facebook.com/cuandoparaamarestarde

https://www.facebook.com/fracasarotriunfartueleccion

TWITTER: @DanielHO

Tell me your name, country where you live and the way you came about this book. Any comment or suggestion, you may contact me by email: daniel.hernandezx1@gmail.com

With love and light"

Daniel Hernández Osorio.

www.ingramcontent.com/pod-product-compliance
Lightning Source LLC
Chambersburg PA
CBHW062206080426
42734CB00010B/1815